# PRIMITIVE AND PEASANT MARKETS

# NEW PERSPECTIVES ON THE PAST

*General Editor*
R. I. Moore

*Advisory Editors*
Gerald Aylmer
Ioan Lewis
David Turley
Patrick Wormald

## PUBLISHED

## IN PREPARATION

# PRIMITIVE
## AND PEASANT MARKETS

## Richard Hodges

Basil Blackwell

First published 1988

Basil Blackwell Ltd
108 Cowley Road, Oxford, OX4 1JF, UK

Basil Blackwell Inc.
432 Park Avenue South, Suite 1503
New York, NY 10016, USA

*British Library Cataloguing in Publication Data*

Hodges, Richard, *1952-*
Primitive and peasant markets.
1. Markets — History
I. Title
381′ .18′ 09    HF5471

ISBN 0-631-14464-1
ISBN 0-631-14465-X Pbk

Typeset in 11 on 13pt Plantin
by DMB (Typesetting), Abingdon, Oxon.
Printed in Great Britain by Billing & Sons Ltd. Worcester

To Colin Renfrew

# Contents

# Editor's Preface

Ignorance has many forms, and all of them are dangerous. In the nineteenth and twentieth centuries our chief effort has been to free ourselves from tradition and superstition in large questions, and from the error in small ones upon which they rest, by redefining the fields of knowledge and evolving in each the distinctive method appropriate for its cultivation. The achievement has been incalculable, but not without cost. As each new subject has developed a specialist vocabulary to permit rapid and precise reference to its own common and rapidly growing stock of ideas and discoveries, and come to require a greater depth of expertise from its specialists, scholars have been cut off by their own erudition not only from mankind at large, but from the findings of workers in other fields, and even in other parts of their own. Isolation diminishes not only the usefulness but the soundness of their labours when energies are exclusively devoted to eliminating the small blemishes so embarrassingly obvious to the fellow-professional on the next patch, instead of avoiding others that may loom much larger from, as it were, a more distant vantage point. Marc Bloch observed a contradiction in the attitudes of many historians: 'when it is a question of ascertaining whether or not some human act has really taken place, they cannot be too painstaking. If they proceed to the reasons for that act, they are content with the merest appearance, ordinarily founded upon one of those maxims of common-place psychology which are neither more nor less true than their opposites.' When the historian peeps across the fence he sees his neighbours, in literature, perhaps, or sociology, just as complacent in relying on historical platitudes which are naive, simplistic or obsolete.

*New Perspectives on the Past* represents not a reaction against specialization, which would be a romantic absurdity, but an attempt to come to terms with it. The authors, of course, are specialists, and their thought and conclusions rest on the foundation of distinguished professional research in different periods and fields. Here they will free themselves, as far as it is possible, from the restraints of subject, region and period within which they ordinarily and necessarily work, to discuss problems simply as problems, and not as 'history' or 'politics' or 'economics'. They will write for specialists, because we are all specialists now, and for laymen, because we are all laymen.

The market is one of the most ubiquitous of human institutions, and it is hardly necessary to insist upon its power to transform the lives of those who produce and consume the goods in which it deals. But it is a power both complex and mysterious, whose operations, as Richard Hodges demonstrates in this remarkably wide-ranging discussion, are not to be understood simply by reiterating the commonplaces of contemporary economics. There are many kinds of market, each associated with particular social conditions and relations as well as particular economic circumstances. The powerful alliance between anthropology and archaeology, between the observer and the spade, enables Hodges to use their markets as windows on past and present worlds, through which we may follow their social and political development with a new and exhilarating intimacy. His book is timely if it helps us to think more clearly about the variety and complexity of ideas and processes whose mere importance is everywhere taken for granted. It is also timely in another way, for its closing chapters show how the acute and pressing difficulties of the 800 million people whose liveliehood depends on the outcome of the bruising and often brutal encounter between their own primitive and peasant marketing systems and those of the developed world are exacerbated by the dogmatic misunderstandings that are bred by bad history. Here is a plain opportunity for a new perspective on the past to help prepare the way for a better perspective in the future.

**R.I. Moore**

# Preface

The market-place rules our lives in more ways than it ever has – or at least, as we approach a new millennium this is how it seems. In these circumstances it is very tempting to interpret past market and exchange systems in the familiar terminology of modern economics. To do this, though, is not only to misunderstand the economics of the past, but the social foundations on which those economies rested. Similarly – and more seriously – one consequence of western capitalism and nationalism has been to expect ex-colonial communities of the so-called Third World to pass swiftly through the economic trajectories which their former colonial masters experienced over a much longer period. At the brink of the twenty-first century we are only just beginning to grasp the error of such thinking. We appear to be far from resolving alternative strategies suitable to the future as opposed to our colonial heyday (cf. Hall, 1985: 247–8). It behoves us now, with a great array of scientific data at our disposal, to understand the space-time dynamics of our global history so that at any one point in time in the future we shall not be induced to make short-term, expedient decisions. Consequently, to understand the history of past markets and to shed light on their place in recent primitive contexts is to arm ourselves intelligently for the future. Unconventional though it has become, the historian should be using the past to define our destiny.

But the markets of the Third World and the markets of our Euro-Asian past are very different phenomena. Daniel Thorner was right to assert in the case of western medieval markets systems that 'Nothing is gained by trying to view *all* peasant economies as variations of that one rather special form. The time has arrived to treat the European experience in categories derived from world history, rather than to squeeze world history into western European categories' (1971: 217). This is why it will be necessary to preface our discussion of peasant markets with discussion, on the face of it rather arid, of competing attempts to systematize their description and classification: as we shall see repeatedly to take terminology for granted is also to take for granted answers to fundamental questions which may be, in fact, quite mistaken.

This book is about aspects of these pre-modern economics, and about certain of those archaic and redundant institutions which continue to exist as expressions of the plight of the Third World. This book, however, is not about economics in the strict sense; rather it is concerned with economic history and its social implications. Its primary focus is the peasant and/or primitive market. This institution is the subject of considerable controversy. First, should we really use the word *peasant*? Second, can any aspect of the market be the exclusive feature of one category of society? Polly Hill has convincingly argued that country people are not peasants (1986: 8–15). I sympathize with her point-of-view: to use terms like countryman or woman does conjure up alternative images, and notably diminishes the connotation of class, oppression and town-county separation that nineteenth-century thinkers infused into a twentieth-century debate. For the purposes of development economics Hill's point is a strong one. But it obfuscates the issue as far as anthropology and history are concerned. So, reluctantly, I have persisted with the term. Similarly, are certain economic conditions exclusive to peasant societies? The great breadth of societies assembled under this title, embracing all the Continents of the world and a multitude of ecological and historical situations makes such a generalization seem spurious in the extreme. Yet if we do not generalize we are left to distinguish between the multitude of types in space and time, and particularism invariably challenges the search for explanation and induces a form of vulgar history. This is clear in the history of the medieval peasant market in the West.

The western medieval variant has been treated either in western (often nationalistic) terms or by anthropologists dependent upon secondary sources couched in this tradition. Global histories like that of Fernand Braudel invariably reduce these economic beginnings to terms they would deem unsatisfactory for the modern world system. As Moses Finley has complained, vulgar positivism exists in the history of ancient towns; by this he means that town-histories are collected and collated but never analyzed (cf. Wacher, 1974). Global approaches demand behavioural analytical techniques that have generalized applicability; space-time dynamics need to be grasped. Geographers like Walter Christaller and today Carol A. Smith have provided us with the tools to come to terms with the spatial implications of these mystifying data. The anthropology of the spatial attributes of peasant markets offers historians enormous insight into social and economic systems. Economic anthropology has likewise developed a great range of concepts appropriate to these needs. Time, too, is now within our grasp. Archaeology has begun to unlock the sequence of economic development in many parts of the world in prehistoric, early historic and historic times. It is a controversial source of data but the modern discipline has equipped itself to investigate not just past elites but their communities as well. In particular, modern archaeology has gained access to historical peasantries in the form of their dwellings, material culture and resource strategies. Above all, the time-depth of archaeology – the embodiment of past behaviour in palimpsests enshrined in towns and the country – make it well-suited to the sweep of Braudelian tempo. The rhythms of time about which the French historians of the *Annales* school have written are fossilized in the material past and can be unlocked, providing we use the right key.

It will be very obvious that I have restricted the scope of this book to those areas with which I am familiar. A great deal of it is devoted to medieval markets, and to some extent updates my earlier study, *Dark Age Economics* (1982). I cannot write confidently about modern markets for these are steeped within capitalist circumstances beyond my grasp. Some sections, however, relate to my experiences in the field where I have had the good fortune to encounter country-people and to question them on their relations to market systems. It will be apparent that the twilight of the South European peasantry has had a profound effect upon me.

I am grateful to Bob Moore, the editor of the series, for inviting me to write this book, for his encouragement while I set to it and for his valuable comments on the first draft. The task was made easier by conversations with my colleague, Robin Torrence and with Chris Wickham. Thankfully neither will approve of the result, for if they did life would be much less stimulating in the future! I should also like to acknowledge my debt to Klavs Randsborg for timely discussions on aspects of this book. Kathleen Biddick kindly sent me offprints pertinent to chapter 5, while chapter 4 contains a good deal from a paper John F. Cherry and I collaborated on, published in *Research in Economic Anthropology* 5 (1983). I am greatly indebted to my wife Debbie for making me the time to write it, as well as for helping to produce the manuscript itself.

I vividly recall the March day on which I became fascinated by economic anthropology and ancient trade in general. Colin Renfrew delivered a lecture on the subject that exceeded even his high standards. His enthusiasm for this subject was lastingly contagious. Therefore, as a small token of this debt, as well as in gratitude for the help and encouragement he has so freely given, I dedicate this book to him.

# 1

# Primitive and Peasant Markets

On market days in Haiti the towns and the country market-
places gather thousands of peasants for hours of busy and noisy
activity. The people come for gossip, courtship and the playing-
out of personal rivalries, to visit a clinic or to register a birth;
but above all they come for business – to sell the tiny surpluses
of their little farms and to buy necessities. They press together
in the ragged lanes among the stalls and the heaps of produce
spread on the ground, inspecting and handling the displays of
textiles, hardware, spices, soap and cooking oils, buying,
selling and chaffering. Children push by hawking trays of
sweets; farmers pull produce-laden animals through the crowds,
calling loudly for the right of way. Trucks back up and turn
around, their drivers honking horns, apparently oblivious of
the people and the great piles of goods. There are vigorous
arguments, sometimes ending in blows and arrests. In the very
intensity of colour, sound and smell the outsider is
overwhelmed with an impression of confusion and disorder.

But for all its apparent anarchy the market place is
characterized by an elaborate underlying order. Wherever they
exist, peasant markets reveal a great deal about the societies
they serve. They are a central economic institution in many
countries where large numbers of small-scale farmers work
their own land. To follow the movement of marketers and
stock through the system is an ideal way to begin to study the
economy and to trace the distribution of economic and
political power in society.

Sidney W. Mintz, 'Peasant Markets'.


The material affluence of nations of the contemporary West is
rooted in its medieval peasant markets and to some extent in

the markets of the Third World in modern times. Markets have played a major role in shaping western history and still play an important if controversial part in the Third World. Market exchange in peasant societies is essentially a pre-capitalist device. In this book, therefore, market exchange denotes relations fused by what Eric R. Wolf has defined as the tributary mode of production. This mode of production functions through the deployment of political power and domination over an agrarian labour force, as opposed to a class division in which one segment of the population produces surpluses and another holds the means of production. Put simply, primitive and peasant markets are and have been attributes of pre-industrial societies in which 80–90 per cent of the population are engaged in full-time agricultural activities.

In this chapter I wish to consider what is meant by primitive and peasant markets. Clearly, these are not simply bustling carnivals of the kind witnessed by Mintz (see p. 1) or visited by package tour parties in the course of summer holidays in underdeveloped countries. As we shall see, primitive and peasant markets have featured in much of man's recent history, especially in the last two millennia. But the market is not an institution congealed in aspic. It has taken different forms, in different environments, in different political circumstances. For this reason anthropologists and historians have debated the definition of markets, sometimes with memorable vigour. These debates about definition may seem 'mind-bogglingly . . . reductionist' today in their oversimplification of the issues (Hart, 1986: 644). But they serve to remind us of how we have arrived at better definitions, and more particularly, they serve to emphasise that such reductionist views can be positively harmful to peoples threatened in some cases, like animals, by extinction (cf. Hill, 1986: 22).

In this chapter, therefore, I wish to set out the anthropological definitions and debates, before considering one profitable avenue for pursuing this subject in the future.

There is no exact definition of this category of exchange, largely because the terms peasant and market embody a range of meanings. The peasant market, therefore, might be positioned on an evolutionary scale between two extreme categories: the 'tribal' exchange-place and the agricultural markets of modern agrarian societies. Of course, 'tribal', peasant and post-peasant modern farmer each have attached to them historical connotations. Each belongs to a social, political and economic context that can be readily distinguished from the other two. Each conjures up in our minds a level of economic development and a certain level of technology. Hence, as George Dalton has pointed out, Charlemagne's serfs in the year 800 were French peasants going to local market-places with a few chickens and eggs; some French citizen-farmers in the year 1900 were also peasants selling some cash crops in regional markets. But the two sorts of French peasant and, in particular, the markets in which each was engaged, differed as of course did the societies, polities, the extent of economic development and the cultural fabric in each.

George Dalton is one of the few anthropologists to have been bold enough to define the peasant market. His definition, however, because he has become the acknowledged doyen of one school of economic anthropology, tends to arouse strong opinions (see below). But his typology of peasant markets like his contentious typology of peasant societies offers a useful starting point. It will be embellished and reshaped in the course of this book.

Dalton first directs our attention to 'what peasant markets were not'. In his opinion they were not aboriginal, indigenous, tribal exchange-places such as those made famous by Bronislav Malinowski in the Trobriand Islands of the Western Pacific (see chapter 2). In these aboriginal contexts, according to Dalton, agriculturalists exchanged yams for wooden bowls with visiting hawker-craftsmen-carvers with whom they had no other economic or social dealings. To the agriculturalists these were petty market exchanges at haggled prices, and the acquired goods were quantitatively insignificant and scarcely important to their livelihoods. This petty marketing occurred in contexts which we would describe as extremely underdeveloped, in which technology was primitive and production barely exceeded domestic requirements. These circumstances, in Wolf's social taxonomy, might be defined as the kin mode of production.

At the other extreme in Dalton's definition are the markets of industrial capitalism. Here, markets are ubiquitous, dominant *foci* that integrate production on an inter-regional and international scale. This market economy reflects a high level (in terms of world history) of achieved economic development and industrial technology. Farmers in such circumstances fall from being 80–90 per cent of the population to about 10–15 per cent. (At 1086, when the Domesday survey of England was compiled almost the same acreage was under plough as that recorded in 1914. In the interval, of course, the population had swelled from about 2–3 millions to about 40 millions.) The agricultural sector becomes an adjunct of the urban industrial, manufacturing sector, as well as the import-export sector of the national economy, integrated with it through markets. As Dalton asserts: 'Here we have total market dependence for livelihood and the ubiquitous use of cash: the self-regulating market economy of Alfred Marshall's *Principles of Economics* [1890]' (Dalton, 1973: 241). Market forces in this sense leave no part of the globe untouched. The industrial capitalist market has been a feature of western history for the past two centuries, and is becoming a feature of world history in the last quarter-century of this millennium.

Now, it should be stressed that this typology is readily criticized: it pigeonholes systems as black or white when each embodies a great range of shades. Nevertheless, we cannot grapple with human history if we have no means to describe it. The definitions may be contentious, but they provide platforms for debate. This has certainly been true of Dalton's other attempts at market typologies.

His first was published jointly with Paul Bohannan as the seminal introduction to their edited volume, *Markets in Africa* (1962). First they defined the market place as a 'specific site where a group of buyers and a group of sellers meet. The market principle is the determination of prices by forces of supply and demand'. The market principle, in their opinion, occurs in three forms which are characteristic of:

1. Societies which lack market-places as such but where the principle is weakly represented.
2. Societies with *peripheral* (my italics) markets – that is, the institution of the market-place is present but the principle does not determine the acquisition of subsistence or the allocation of land and labour resources.
3. Societies dominated by a market principle and the price mechanism.

In addition to these definitions of market-places, George Dalton has proposed at least three different types of peasant markets which he classifies as follows:

1. Traditional peasant markets
2. Peasant markets in early modern and pre- (or proto) industrial societies.
3. Hybrid/composite peasant markets.

A fourth category, arising from transplanted peasants such as the French in Quebec and the Dutch in South Africa, to some extent over-complicates the scheme.

1. *Traditional peasant markets*, in Dalton's view, are those found in Western Europe up until the Late Middle Ages, and in Japan before about AD 1600. Dalton allows for the historical variation within this broad category, admitting that markets in England at 1066 were different in several respects from those operating in the fourteenth century. Despite these distinctions 'the larger economies were overwhelmingly agricultural, typically three-fourths or more of the population directly engaged in agriculture, and, of course, underdeveloped in technology and low in output per capita produced' (Dalton, 1973: 241). He sums up this society as one where:

more than half of all output produced was *not* transacted by market sale; that is, most of what was produced was consumed directly by the peasant farmers' households or by priests and lords to whom the peasants - freemen as well as serfs - made obligatory payments. The rest was sold for cash in four sorts of controlled output markets:

1. market-places in villages and hamlets, usually meeting weekly . . .
2. urban market-places to supply foodstuffs and raw materials to tradesmen and craftsmen, who, in turn sold some fabricated goods to peasants and for export;
3. foreign market trade in staples, wool and wine;
4. periodic large-scale fairs (international market-places).

Dalton asserts that these markets were controlled by political, municipal or guild authorities. They were designed for produced goods (commodities in the terminology of many anthropologists (e.g. Gregory, 1982)) and raw materials rather than, for example, land and labour, which were relatively minor features of these market exchanges.

2. *Peasant markets in early modern and proto-industrial societies*, according to Dalton are those such as occurred in Western Europe between the fourteenth, and late nineteenth centuries, and in Japan from about 1600 to 1914. They were partly modern and partly traditional. The ranked existence of a range of regional and international markets began to determine more specialized peasant agrarian production. Peasants, similarly, purchased some commodities rather than making or producing them themselves. Such societies were still categorized by 'a good deal of farm production for peasant household consumption', and by frequent use of out-of-date technology.

3. *Hybrid/composite peasant market systems* appeared in most parts of the World following colonization by West European nations and the development of cash-cropping schemes by planters. These economies 'combine economic and social characteristics from medieval European peasantry, early and late modernization; in short a very mixed bag of peasantries with a very mixed bag of markets, running the whole gamut from tribal to post-peasant' (Dalton, 1973: 242).

To repeat, Dalton's catch-all definitions provide a useful point of departure. As he writes: 'The only *general* meaning to be attached to the term "peasant market" is negative: that they are not the moneyless petty markets of aboriginal Melanesia and that they are not the full-blooded input and output markets of late nineteenth-century industrial Britain' (1973: 242).

Not unexpectedly George Dalton's classification of markets, like his approach to aboriginal economics and peasants, has aroused a good deal of criticism. Eric R. Wolf, for example, has firmly challenged Dalton's 'sequential' typology of peasants upon which this categorization of markets is based. Wolf makes three forceful criticisms of Dalton's typology of peasant societies, which apply equally to his views on peasant markets. These were:

1. that the traditional peasantry of medieval Europe is itself but the outcome of a process of hybridization of tribal groups after the disintegration of the Roman empire;
2. that Dalton vastly overschematizes the diversity of conditions characteristic of Western Europe during any phase of its existence;
3. that Dalton pays too little attention to the degree to which European expansion determined the development or lack of development of societies elsewhere in the world, and the extent to which European growth was predicated upon the establishment of hybrid/composite peasant systems (Wolf, 1972: 410).

From another standpoint Polly Hill (1986: 55) has charged Bohannan and Dalton's scheme with lacking a perspective of market-based societies over a long time-period. Furthermore, in common to some degree with Wolf, she charges them with failing to address the question of colonialism as they sought to chart the evolution of markets. Like Wolf's criticisms, these may be justified but nevertheless, as we shall see, these typologies in fact prove valuable once we have explored sound multi-disciplinary sources on the evolution of markets. The alternatives are far less convincing.

One alternative is to challenge the validity of generalizations; to discuss economic systems as regionally idiosyncratic and to focus on comparisons of one region with another. Another, more familiar, alternative is to concentrate upon markets as facets of general behavioural integration. Typical of this approach is Marvin Harris' definition of markets in his popular textbook on anthropology:

marketplaces occur in rudimentary form wherever groups of non-kin and strangers assemble and trade one item for another. Among band and village peoples, marketplace trading usually involves the barter of one valuable consumable item for another: fish for yams, coconuts for axes; and so forth. In this type of market, before the development of all-purpose money, only a limited range of goods and services is exchanged. The great bulk of exchange transactions takes place outside of the marketplace and continue to involve various forms of reciprocity and redistribution. With the development of all-purpose money, however, price-making exchanges come to dominate all other forms of exchange. . . . Virtually everything that is produced or consumed comes to have a price, and buying and selling become a major cultural preoccupation. . . . Price-market exchanges are notable for the anonymity and impersonality of the exchange process and stand in contrast to the personal and kin-based exchanges of pre-state economies (Harris, 1980: 238).

In Marvin Harris' opinion, the market is a place and a spirit. There are markets where exchange regulations *appear* to be flexible, and other more complex markets where all-purpose money is employed as a medium to regulate values. There are markets which occur on the periphery of primitive economies; and there are those which are an integral part of complex societies. One point is common to all the various types of this institution, wherever it occurs: markets are a feature of exchange beyond the kin-group.

Caught between the palaeolithic quality of stone age economics and the manipulation of capital, primitive and peasant market systems became prey to a debate in the fifties

and sixties between two strident schools of economic anthropology: the formalists and the substantavists. As Dalton is
perhaps the most prolific exponent of the latter school and
Harris inclines towards the former it is appropriate to specify
briefly what divides these protagonists.

The debate was between those who believed the received
wisdom of formal economics was universally valid – the
formalists – and those who held that production-distribution
processes in primitive and peasant societies operate on totally
different principles – the substantivists. The formalists held
that supply and demand factors, issues of modern classical
economics, could be applied to primitive societies. (It is an
assumption often made, for example, by historians of first
millennium A.D. economics.) By contrast, the substantivists,
influenced by social thinkers like Max Weber (cf. Hart, 1986:
644), argued that social conditions often qualified what might
to us seem economically rational. In other words, exchange in
many pre-industrial societies was guided, as often as not, by
social conventions aimed at securing the cohesion of the group
as opposed to economic self-interest.

The debate can be traced back to the works of Bronislav
Malinowski (centering upon his Trobriand Island research)
and Marcel Mauss, the student of Emile Durkheim, best
known for his celebrated book *The Gift*. Both scholars sought
to demonstrate the complex forms of trade and exchange in
primitive societies. Published shortly after the end of the First
World War, their works mark the end of nineteenth-century
ethnocentricism on socio-economic issues in anthropology.
But it was Karl Polanyi, a rather unorthodox economist, who
formulated the substantivist school as such. Polanyi was an
East European emigré who became interested in economic
anthropology late in his life. His most famous volume is *Trade
and Markets in Archaic Societies*, which he edited, and to
which he contributed a seminal essay entitled 'The economy
as instituted process'. In this essay Polanyi advances the view
that 'the substantive meaning of economic derives from man's
dependence for his living upon nature and his fellows. It

refers to the interchange with his natural and social environment, insofar as this results in supplying him with the means of material want - satisfaction' (1957: 243). By contrast, 'the formal meaning of economic derives from the logical character of the means-ends relationship, as apparent in such words as "economical" or "economizing". It refers to a definite situation of choice, namely, that between the different uses of means induced by an insufficiency of those means. If we call the rules governing choice of means the logic of rational action, then we may denote this variant of logic, with an improvised term, as formal economics' (Polanyi, 1957: 243).

The economic typology outlined in this essay proved an important contribution to economic anthropology, generating the nub of the debate. Polanyi's typology consisted of three forms of economic process: reciprocity, redistribution and (market) exchange. Reciprocity, he defined as exchange or interaction between individuals or groups of broadly similar standing. Redistribution, by contrast, designates the role of some central agent or agency in handling exchange between individuals or groups. Polanyi implied that this agent or agency was appropriating some portion of that handled. Market exchange in his view involved everybody, each person finding his own level in which to interact within this all-embracing system.

Polanyi's work, both in abstract and empirical terms, has been developed by his students. Most notable amongst these have been Marshall Sahlins and George Dalton. Sahlins, for example, has argued in the preface of his influential book *Stone Age Economics* that the decisive differences between formalism and substantivism are ideological. Formal economics embodies as axiomatic the categories of the western liberal tradition in which it evolved, and flourishes as ideology at home and ethnocentrism abroad. Unlike substantivism, it draws great strength from its profound compatibility with bourgeois society (Sahlins, 1974: xiii–xiv).

Dalton has addressed the same themes: 'the absence of machine technology, pervasive market organization and all-purpose money, plus the fact that economic transactions cannot be understood apart from social obligations, create, as it were a non-Euclidian universe to which Western economic theory cannot be fruitfully applied' (1961: 20). More specifically, Sahlins rejects the existence of 'infinite needs' in primitive economies. The demand for material goods, in his opinion, is highly inelastic and 'depends on the social structure of the trade relation' (1974: 313). Dalton's definition of peasant economics concurs with this. Put more fully, Dalton often subscribes to Eric R. Wolf's definition of this type of economy:

the peasant aims at subsistence, not reinvestment. The starting point of the peasant is the needs which are defined by his culture. His answer, the production of cash crops for a market is prompted largely by his inability to meet these needs within the sociocultural segment of which he is a part. He sells cash crops to get money, but this money is used in turn to buy goods and services which he requires to subsist and to maintain his social status, rather than to enlarge his scale of operations. We may thus draw a line between the peasant and another agricultural type whom we call the "farmer". The farmer views agriculture as a business enterprise. He begins his operations with a sum of money which he invests in a farm. The crops produced are sold not only to provide goods and services for the farm operator but to permit amortization and expansion of his business. The aim of the peasant is subsistence. The aim of the farmer is reinvestment (Wolf, 1955: 454).

There were opponents of this standpoint long before Polanyi's historic contribution to the subject. Formalists like Raymond Firth and Marshall Herskovits had challenged the Malinowski/Mauss approach soon after it was formulated. They were suspicious of the special conceptual frameworks invented for pre-capitalist societies, in no small measure because of the ethnocentrism they believed to be embodied in such approaches. In 1939, for example, Raymond Firth asserted:

What is required from primitive economics is the analysis of material from uncivilized communities in such a way that it will be directly comparable with the material of modern economics, matching assumption with assumption and so allowing generalizations to be ultimately framed which will subsume the phenomena of both civilized and uncivilized, price and non-price communities into a body of principles about human behaviour which will be truly universal (1939: 29).

Firth illustrates this thesis in his book *Malay Fishermen: Their Peasant Economy* (1946) and in his seminal essay on 'Capital, Saving and Credit in Peasant Societies' (1964). In each he makes use of mainstream economics to shed light upon peasant systems. (In his essay on credit, for example, he briefly dwells upon a Keynesian model to interpret Muslim attitudes to this issue (1964: 33).) But following Polanyi's essay on the substantivist-formalist approaches, and in particular the works of Bohannan, Dalton and Sahlins (to name a few) several pronounced attacks, often sharp in their rhetoric were made upon the substantivists by those following the contrary creed. Many of these critics were engaged in field research upon Third World peasantries and detected the invasion of modern economic problems even at the household level within what Robert Redfield defined as 'Little Community' studies.

A central theme of the formalist thesis is that supply and demand do exist in all primitive and peasant societies. Foragers, for example, adopt strategies to optimize their resources if they can, and gladly respond to the prospects of an increase if it can be had without excessive effort. The Russian economist Alexander Chayanov made the same point in his studies of the Russian peasantry in the 1920s:

Of course, our critics are free to understand the labour-consumer balance theory as a sweet little picture of the Russian peasantry in the likeness of the moral French peasants, satisfied with everything and living like the birds of the air. We, ourselves, do not have such a conception and are inclined to believe that no peasant would refuse either good roast beef, or a gramophone, or even a block of Shell Oil Company shares, if the chance occurred. Unfortunately, such chances do not present themselves in large numbers, and the peasant family wins every kopek by hard, intensive toil. And in these circumstances, they are obliged not only to do without shares and a gramophone, but sometimes without beef as well (1966, [1925]: 47-8).

The thrust of Chayanov's thesis is that desire may be present but need not be translated into demand because the outlay in terms of a peasant's time, energy, money may well amount to extra drudgery. Chayanov illustrated his thesis with a great deal of evidence, some of which has recently been subject to a good deal of critical reappraisal. Nevertheless, his central ideas challenged the economic strategy of Russia in the thirties and he paid the ultimate price for his views in the political purges of that era. Much of the debate focussed upon how an economic system changed gear, becoming a new system. Why do primitive societies characterized by a kin-based mode of production enter into trade and exchange? How does market exchange come about? The answers to such questions clearly are not to be found in the oversimplifications thrashed out in the debate. Marshall Sahlins, for instance, acknowledged the incidence of supply and demand factors in primitive economies, and attributes the beginnings of regional exchange to trade partnerships between otherwise autonomous groupings. In this respect he does not differ much from Karl Marx who pinpointed the importance of trade as a trigger for primitive economies. According to Sahlins:

In primitive trade, the path to economic equilibrium lay not across the play of autonomous individuals or firms fixing a price through the parallel contentions of buyers and sellers. It began rather from the interdiction of competition within the community of either, traversed a structure of institutional arrangements that with varying facility brought together partners mutually obliged to be generous, upon separating those not so inclined, to negotiate in the end an analogous "price". The similarity to market trade appears when abstraction is made of all this – and of the protracted space-time scale, perhaps in reality a changeover of decades from trade with one ethnic group to partnership in another. Then the primitive system, globally considered, does bring those particular persons into relations of trade, and at those rates, as reasonably reflect the availability and utility of goods (1974: 314).

The substantivist-formalist debate has waned in the past decade. One reason for this may be the ascendency of economic thinking in our present times. The science of economics, with all its arithmetic calculations induces the arbiter to think twice about the woolier notions encapsulated in the substantivist treatises. Consequently, many of those sympathetic to the substantivist school have been wooed by the French neo-Marxists, of whom Maurice Godelier is the most renowned exponent. Godelier accepts the substantivist criticism of the formalists, but goes much further (1977). He wants a general theory of modes of production going beyond the surface issues. Like Levi-Strauss, Godelier places a good deal of weight on the cognitive as a structuring aspect of the modes of production. The problem with his work, and those affiliated to him, is that the abstractions mask the merit of his logic. The original debate, while simpler and perhaps cruder in quality highlights the essence of a problem in studying primitive economics which at an abstract level, at least, still merits consideration by historians. A useful step to address the central issues has recently been published by John H. Dowling.

John H. Dowling accepts the process Sahlins describes but challenges the notion of generosity underpinning the critical change in a community's resource strategy. Drawing upon a wide range of ethnographic data he points to self-interest being as common a guiding principle as altruism. When military opportunities avail themselves, for example, self-interest frequently adopts a more naked, brutal appearance. Dowling, accordingly, finds three axioms (as he terms them) which not only bridge the main features of the two schools of economic anthropology, but also embrace the current thinking of structural Marxists whose research is becoming increasingly important in this field (Bloch 1983). These axioms can be summarized as follows:

1. All peoples have infinitely expandable wants and . . . all people are motivated by self-interest and are guided to some extent by rational decision-making.
2. There are economy-specific assumptions which have explanatory utility in certain conditions but not in

others. The social relations pertaining to gift exchange, commodity exchange and capitalism each take a different form.

3. The market will take a form dependent upon regional characteristics (Dowling 1980: 293).

Dowling ranks these three axioms as primary, secondary and tertiary assumptions. He believes that the substantivists have denied the primary assumption, while the formalists appear to be mistaken in holding that both primary and secondary assumptions have universal applicability. He points out that the two sides have been arguing past one another – a feature of so many academic debates. 'In fact', asserts Dowling, 'the two perspectives complement one another.' Sahlins too, was striving towards this position in *Stone Age Economics* as he attempted to explain the existence of supply and demand curves operating within aboriginal exchange networks. Maximizing resources is a feature of most primitive societies. Nevertheless, social parameters determine the form and development of exchange systems in pre-capitalist conditions. Rigid approaches to such societies are bound to reduce their economics to a set of false formulae.

The legitimacy of this argument becomes clearer once we can grasp the formation and development of peasant market systems using data that has temporal and spatial depth. The anthropologist trapped in his own time, like the historian trapped by the sample of written material, is at a disadvantage working in isolation on these kinds of economies. Like state formation, the making of market systems can best be traced by a multiplicity of sources. The results, it may be safely contended, steer the issue of markets beyond the bounds of the 'dismal science' and safely into the realms of mainstream socio-economic history. The 'mind-bogglingly . . . reductionist' aspects of these debates, therefore, while perhaps no longer strictly relevant, have nonetheless helped to clarify the position, and have enabled us to examine more exacting approaches to primitive and peasant economics.

## Models of Social Reality

> Spatial models are the charts upon which social reality is
> projected, and through which it may become at least partially
> clear; they are truly models for all the different movements of
> time, and for all categories of social life.
>
> Fernand Braudel *On History*.

Spatial models offer an alternative means of defining economies. These enable the anthropologist and historian to define
production and distribution at a regional level in a way which
is quite familiar to us today as we are guided through the daily
television news. But as we have just seen, applying modern
criteria to interpret the economics of past societies is fraught
with problems. In this section, therefore, I wish to set out how
a number of spatial and anthropological concepts enable the
historian to advance beyond the problems of definition
encountered, for example, in the Polanyi debate.

Geographers have been engaged in spatial analysis since
industrialisation altered the configurations of the European
landscape. As early as 1826 Johann von Thunen published a
spatial model based upon a law of diminishing returns with
distance which more recently Chisholm has translated into a
land use model (1968). This is currently termed site-
catchment analysis by archaeologists who have endeavoured
to show that sites may often be strategically positioned to
make advantageous use of roughly circular territories between
2 and 5 km, in diameter. (The concept is open to a good deal
of criticism and has to be employed with caution.) Possibly the
most influential of these models has been Walter Christaller's
central-place theory (1966). Christaller observed that sites
achieve the most efficient and advantageous relationship to
one another by being distributed in a hexagonal pattern; when
the size of one territory, or the number and variety of sites
served by its central places changes, corresponding changes

tend to occur in the other territories to preserve the hexagonal pattern by reorienting it.

Christaller's model is dependent upon two principle assumptions:

1. The population and (thus the) purchasing power are distributed over an undifferentiated and unbounded surface;
2. Maximization of profits and minimization of costs (supply and demand) are regulated in some way through a structured market system existing in this space.

Christaller's model like von Thunen's, however, lays great emphasis upon maximizing benefits. Each assumes that the producers not only wish to maximize output, but are in the position to do so. In many respects these could be described as formalist models. The archaeologist David Clarke challenged the suitability of such models for primitive and peasant societies, and argued that models appropriate to these economies were needed (1977: 23–4). Coincidentally, models of exactly this form were being devised by two different schools of anthropologists. Jonathon Friedman and Michael Rowlands (1978) presented a wide-ranging structural Marxist appraisal of the spatial characteristics of pre-state societies. They developed their typology as an 'epigenetic evolutionary scheme' in which certain of Marx's criteria are explicitly modified. The scheme, however, employs spatial models only in an abstract sense.

By contrast, the work of Carol A. Smith, working in the tradition of South American peasant studies by Mintz and Wolf (cf. Silverman, 1979), approaches this issue by employing not only certain of Marx's criteria but also Christaller's spatial formulae. Smith pays particular attention to class relations within, as well as beyond, the regions with which she is concerned. Smith's work, in my opinion, offers a powerful

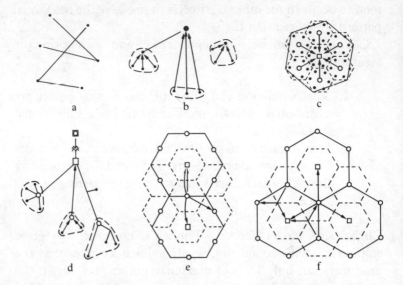

**Figure 1** *Carol A. Smith's model: (a) an unbounded network system where exchange in the region is direct and no division of labour exists; (b) a bounded hierarchical system where exchange in the region may be controlled by some central authority, but where the production and distribution of commodities is low; (c) a solar central-place system where an administered market exists in the region, maintaining a low level of commodity production and distribution, and an equally low level of social stratification; (d) a dendritic central-place system in which a monopolistic market (gateway community) occurs on the edge of the region to control prestige goods exchange and the production of limited commodities for external distribution; (e), and (f) two variants of central-place systems in which interlocking competitive markets generate a high level of production and distribution in a well-regulated socio-economic system.*
*Source: Smith, 1976a.*

tool for analyzing primitive and peasant systems and merits detailed appraisal in this context. In the following pages I shall summarize her innovative spatial models, and also offer a few criticisms. Thereafter, in subsequent chapters, I shall use her ideas to shed light on a variety of historical examples.

Smith's approach might be best described as anthropological geography. It might also be defined as a qualified neo-Marxist one in which she maintains that economic stratification is a defining characteristic of agrarian societies. She also accepts Marx's explanation that the forces and relations of production structure differential control of the means of production. Accordingly, in her view, economic classes are defined in terms of access to or control over the means of production. But she emphatically contends that agrarian societies exist where control of the means of production does not provide the basis for stratification. Instead she seeks to assert that stratification in agrarian societies results 'from differential access to or control over the means of exchange; variations in stratification systems is related to types of exchange between producers and non-producers as they affect and are affected by the spatial distribution of the elite and the level of commercialisation in the region and beyond' (Smith, 1976a: 310).

Her models, it might be claimed, offer a corollary to the maximization models described above and are, therefore, appropriate to pre-capitalist social formulations. Smith points out, however, that most exchanges occurring across social divisions tend to be imbalanced. As a result she differs from the substantivists who maintained that some social commodity such as spiritual or physical protection, for example, might balance the exchange of gifts or commodities (1976: 312). Imbalanced exchange in her opinion, is a distinguishing feature of stratified agrarian societies, and the economic status of the elite is seen to depend upon their control of distribution and exchange rather than production.

Smith's model embodies a typology which takes into account three frameworks (reminiscent of Bohannan and Dalton's definitions of markets (see above)). These are:

1. Uncommercialized exchange (*nonmarket exchange*) where transactions are 'direct';
2. partially commercialized, noncompetitive exchange (*controlled market exchange*) where transactions are administered (by the elite);
3. fully commercialized exchange (*competitive market exchange*).

These exchange types are as follows (see figure 1.1):

1. An 'unbounded network system' where exchange is direct and no division of labour exists. This is an uncommercialized system found usually in aboriginal contexts. Small quantities of simple resources (e.g. stones for axes, certain foodstuffs) tend to figure in such networks, invariably gaining value as these are taken further from their source.

2. A 'bounded hierarchical network' system where exchange is direct, and in which the division of labour is slight. The system is uncommercialized with only the movement of scarce or prestige resources. Smith contends that this system typifies many feudal societies in which power is based upon landed wealth.

3. A 'solar central-place system' in which an administered market exists at the centre of the region. In this system the division of labour is slight, and the network of relationships between the central-place and satellite settlements is determined principally by administrative/decision-making forces. The system as a result is only partially commercialized.

4. A 'dendritic central-place system' in which a monopolistic market (a gateway community or port-of-trade (see chapter 2) occurs on the confines of a region. (Smith's term, dendritic, is meant to convey the tree-like pattern of exchange relations within the region. The monopolistic market represents the base of the tree-trunk, while each branch connects an elite site to many smaller places.) This is a partially commercialized system in which exchange with another region is encouraged, but significantly is concentrated in a single centre (gateway community). The items obtained in this exchange are employed by the elite to sustain or sometimes to manipulate the social system. One feature of the system is a limited increase in craft specialization at the monopolistic single centre (gateway community) which has some influence upon a zone from which that community draws its subsistence. Smith contends that these systems occur on the periphery of what Immanuel Wallerstein has called world systems (1974: 15) (see below: p. 30). Following Wallerstein, Smith believes

that gateway communities indicate an exploitative, imbalanced exchange.

5. 'Interlocking central-place' systems in which competitive markets are a prominent feature. In these systems a high division of labour exists, and the implementation of tributary relations to mediate across the divisions means that the market fully extends to all parts of the region. Essentially these correspond to Christaller's models in which maximization of profits and minimization of costs are the norm.

In sum, Smith believes that uncommercialized exchange occurs in the 'unbounded network system'; partially commercialized exchange distinguishes the 'bounded network', 'solar central-place' and 'dendritic central-place' systems; and fully commercialized exchange occurs in 'interlocking central-place systems. Her models can be summarised as shown in table 1.1.

**Table 1.1** *Correlates of Carol A. Smith's regional models*

|  | Settlement hierarchy | Production | Distribution |
| --- | --- | --- | --- |
| 1. Unbounded network | No hierarchy | Minimal | Minimal |
| 2. Bounded hierarchical network | Minimal hierarchy | Minimal: at elite sites | Minimal: between elites |
| 3. Solar central-place | Large elite sites/ for administrative/ ideological purposes | Focused at central-place; otherwise minimal | Minimal |
| 4. Dendritic central-place | Monopolistic trading sites and limited elite hierarchy | Large-scale at trading site; otherwise low level of production | Plentiful at trading site; limited at elite sites |
| 5. Interlocking central-place | Hierarchy of competitive markets | High-level production at all levels of hierarchy | Distribution focused on market hierarchy |

For reasons implicit in the earlier part of this chapter it will be clear that Smith's typology cannot be used as straight-forwardly as table 1.1 implies. Her model, after all, is based upon her research in modern Guatamala. In other words her theory relates principally to pre-capitalist contexts, while she appears to have in mind those peasant circumstances in the present Third World in which a global economy affects and is affected by Gautamalan peasants (cf. Smith, 1984). Accordingly, some aspects of her work require qualification. I would propose, therefore, the following amendments to her typology:

1. Smith places undue emphasis upon exchanges which *appear* to be imbalanced. In this respect she remains close to traditional Marxist thinking, putting emphasis upon exchange as exploitation of one group by another. In nonmarket and controlled market exchange (as Smith defines them) a primary function of exchange is to obtain goods which are used in cycles of gift-giving (what Polanyi defined as reciprocity) to maintain the status quo. This point is of considerable significance for dendritic central-place systems because they do not occur exclusively in colonial situations. European examples exist, as we shall see in the following chapters, of two comparable powers engaging in exchange at monopolistic centres in which the balance of trade was critical to both parties. In these circumstances the traditional Marxist approach takes little account of the significance of the exchange for both parties and therefore fails to appreciate its role in social reproduction. This is an issue of some importance, as we shall see in chapters 2 and 3, and throws into relief the difference between partially commercialized and fully commercialized systems. In her original essays setting out her model Smith briefly acknowledges the impact of world systems (see below for a discussion of these) through a monopolistic central-place in a dendritic system. But she assumes that world systems cause increased production, which generate periodic markets within the region in order to supply the monopolistic centre, which in turn become fixtures as competitive markets. This

economistic equation reduces the producing society to a secondary parameter.

More recently, however, Smith has written an important critique of this issue illustrating how global systems have affected and have been affected by Guatemala over the past century (1984). In this essay she shows that the circumstances in Guatemala cannot be lumped together with other Central American states in arguments about global economic policy. Guatemala, she contends, has a very different history from countries like El Salvador. Essentially it was the only republic in the region to develop a dense, competitive, rural marketing system whose traders were almost entirely rural peasants. Secondly, a complex social structure evolved in Guatemala. In particular, unlike other Central American states, regional elites had no local landed power base, and thus possessed little economic power over the peasantry. Thirdly, all the urban population growth and most economic infrastructure became concentrated in one city. Only Costa Rica developed a comparable top-heavy urban system in the region. Taking these elements as a starting-point, Smith proceeds to show how foreign policy - global political decision-making - has failed to appreciate the regional socio-economic circumstances. 'The dialectic of global and local forces must be considered to understand the nature and progress of world capitalism itself' (1984: 224). Simple dominance theory inherent in the world systems approach is often too bald and reductionist in its effects. In particular, it pays too little attention to the social circumstances which generate the economic strategies. I shall return to this issue in subsequent chapters.

2. Another qualification of Smith's models is that there exist variations of several of her models which reveal that she sets great store by political control but fails to describe what happens when control is fragmented rather than centralized. For example, the dendritic central-place system depends upon a strong centralized authority. But where political power in the region is shared by many members of the elite, there will

exist several, possibly many, overlapping dendritic systems. Examples of the two, contrasting types of dendritic systems are known from Middle Saxon England. These are described in chapter 2. Similar political competition might lead to regions consisting of a patchwork quilt of solar central-place systems as opposed to one major centre. Spatial patterns of this kind occur in Carolingian Europe as well as the Abbasid Orient, as is described in chapter 2.

3. Finally as Smith acknowledges, competitive market systems may take several forms. In fact, examples of fully commercialized systems functioning through a solar central-place are well-known where the main consideration is the provision of efficient administration or the exercise of effective territorial control. Similarly, commercialized dendritic central-place systems are well-documented where a hierarchy of commercialized centres can be identified, but their functional importance diminishes progressively with increasing distance from the monopolistic, highest-order centre.

How are we to distinguish between the partially commercialized and fully commercialized variants - between, for example, the two kinds of solar central-place patterning in a region? The distinction between the two patterns must be found in the degree to which maximization of benefits and minimization of costs determine site location. In addition, lower order markets would be expected in the fully commercialized system as would other signs of relatively more advanced production, distribution and consumption such as the mass-replication of standardized goods, exploitation of optimum agrarian resources, and ranked distribution of goods according to market value. Such features would be absent or no more than incipient in partially commercialized regional systems.

These qualifications apart, Smith's work amounts to an impressive model for identifying the spatial attributes of primitive and peasant economies. It would be wrong to imply that these models are exclusive; other patterns must have existed in world history. Nevertheless, this typology includes modern anthropological data as well as modern geographical information; for this it must be applauded. The most major reservation, of course, is that like maps the models amount to a series of static expressions. The past was rarely so static, and accordingly in any implementation of Smith's thesis the dynamics of long-term change need to be borne in mind. These dynamics will be the subject of later chapters in this book. At this point the historian will be wondering, instead, whether data exist with which we can realistically test these models.

## Making Maps

> It is a salutary experience for the local historian to draw a detailed map of his area. The map is a remarkably uncompromising medium for conveying information. When he writes, the historian will obviously write a lot about the things he knows and much less about the things he does not know. Whether deliberately or not, he will usually avoid drawing attention to the gaps in his knowledge, leaving his readers, and often himself, with the impression that he knows more than he really does, and that the gaps are unimportant or even nonexistent. It gives equal emphasis to every part of the whole and there can be no sliding over doubtful points.
>
> Harvey, 'Mapping the Village'.

Charting social and economic reality poses a real problem for the historian. If spatial models are important measures for all the different movements of time and for all categories of social life, what is the historian to do? Maps, of course, exist in some number for antiquity and from the later Middle Ages in Europe, and explorers and colonisers prepared good renditions of Africa and Asia in more recent centuries. But these documents are often not sufficient to reconstruct the scale and character of these significant, if transitory, economic stages. The historical image of the economic past, therefore, is derived largely from sources compiled when proto-capitalist and fully industrialized societies existed. As Harvey notes, there can be no sliding over this point. It is difficult to measure social and economic reality when the historian is dependent upon those who made history and has no means of quantifying those for whom history has been denied. As we shall see in the case of early medieval markets, the historical 'image' and spatial reality seldom concur.

Anthropology and archaeology in their different forms are important complementary sources of information for the historian pursuing this economic issue. Anthropologists and archaeologists work most successfully with regional spatial units, focussing upon sample communities, and thereafter very often upon sample units (households) within these communities. Anthropologists, of course, concentrate upon a single 'time-slice', while the real merits of archaeology lie in its time-depth. The evaluation of their data has been made possible by borrowing analytical models from geographers, some of which were described in the previous section. Many distinguished analytical approaches to spatial data (either of a modern or fossilized form) are now available but one particular technique pertinent to identifying different market types merits a brief mention.

The technique in question is known as the rank-size rule. It is an empirical generalization well-suited to assessing mapped patterns at the coarsest levels. Its importance lies in emphasizing the relationships inherent in regional constellations of settlements. The rule notes that settlement systems often have a population size distribution such that when these places are ranked in descending order by population size, a place of rank $r$ has a population equal to $l/r$ that of the largest settlement in the system. This relationship is lognormally distributed so that a linear plot is produced when the results are set out on a logarithmic graph. Several explanations for this have been proposed, but some debate exists about the precise reasons for it. Several scholars have suggested that it is a product of a highly integrated urbanized system, and a classic expression of Christaller's central-place theory (described

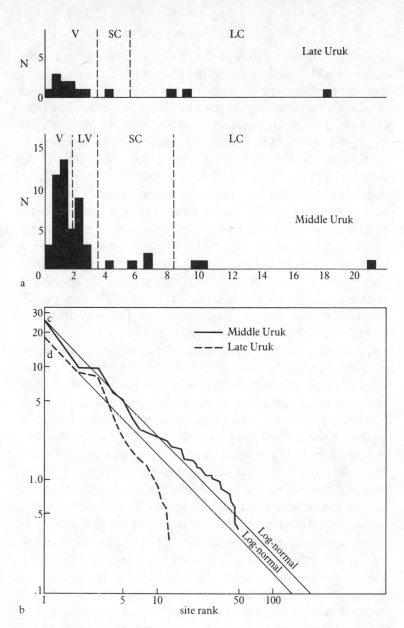

**Figure 2** *Rank-size distributions of Middle and Late Uruk settlements (c.3500–3150 BC) on the Susiana Plain of south-west Iran. (a) Site histograms divided up into villages (V), large villages (LV), small centres (SC) and large centres (LC); and (b) logarithmic plot of site size against site rank.*
*Source: Johnson, 1975 & 1977.*

above). Of greater interest to the questions under review here are cases which deviate from this pattern.

One type of deviation has been termed a *primate* distribution in which a logarithmic plotting of settlement size against rank produces a markedly nonlinear, *concave* plot. In other words, large places exceed their predicted size or *vice versa*, and small settlements are smaller than anticipated (Blanton, 1976; Johnson, 1977). This type of pattern crudely corresponds to either the dendritic or solar central-place systems in which competitive forces are minimized through monopolistic control of an urban community. A second type of deviation produces the opposite result: a markedly convex plot on a logarithmic graph. In these cases large settlements are smaller than expected, while the smaller places are larger. This is not as common a feature of the West, though J. C. Russell (1972) claims that it occurred in later medieval Tuscany. It is also typical of pre-Roman Iron Age Europe.

Rank-size patterning, therefore, expresses different sociopolitical relationships as well as economic interactions, albeit in an often oversimplified form. Given historical data as well as either anthropological or archaeological measures these relationships can be defined much more closely. The integration of the central-place hierarchy with its linear plot may be contrasted with the concave and convex plots indicative of alternative ways of managing space. As a form of analysis rank-size patterning amounts to the first stage in a multi-stage analytical strategy. The second stage needs to focus upon the community and its use of space. There are a number of studies which have successfully made use of the distinction between public and private space, and their various dependent variations. Analyses of these kinds establish the significance of public/ritual monuments against, for instance, productive units within a centre. Likewise a third stage of analysis defines the use of space by household units using similar criteria.

Spatial analyses, of course, are only one dimension of 'how it was'. In many respects the map, so-to-speak, is a chart upon which reality can be constructed. Studies of production, distribution and consumption provide insights on the processes determining these spatial attributes. Cultural expressions ranging from ritual to art provide a third measure of social interaction in these circumstances. The past, in short, has spatial rhythms just as it has temporal rhythms.

Maps, though, often embody a highly segregated awareness of the world. Nineteenth-century nationalism and colonialism have seduced us into accepting regions or states as natural units which function in glorious isolation. Nothing, of course, is further from the truth. In a study of market systems we must begin by recognizing that man is *par excellence* a highly mobile creature. Students of Early Man have now demonstrated extraordinary continental connections in Palaeolithic and Mesolithic times. Marco Polo, as a consequence, was merely part of a more-or-less continuous chain of connections linking the European and Asian continents for at least 10,000 years. Markets, therefore, must be viewed in inter-regional as well as regional terms. In this respect history must slip its often deceitful nineteenth-century chains and council wisdom as far as modern North-South circumstances are concerned.

Marx and his followers, of course, have always paid special attention to theories of global dominance. Most of Marx's energy was spent on efforts to understand the history and workings of capitalism. In his opinion, to understand the modern world we must trace the growth of the world market and the course of capitalist development. Two modern scholars have developed Marx's thesis on these matters: André Gunder Frank and Immanuel Wallerstein.

André Gunder Frank, an economist, is best known for his trenchant attacks on the tendency to see Third World economies solely in terms of their 'progress' towards modernisation on the western model (1966). Frank argued in fierce rebuttals of American economists that development and underdevelopment were not separate phenomena, but were closely connected. Capitalism, in short, in some form or other affected all parts of the globe. He identified an exploitative relationship between metropolitan centres and dependent satellites. In his view, capitalism distorted and thwarted the development of these satellites to its own benefit. Exponents of this dependency theory, as it has become known, have fiercely attacked those economists who set up the western tradition as a model for future global economies. The Brandt commission on International Development Issues stems to some extent from the work of Frank and his associates.

Dependency theory has been developed by the historian and sociologist Immanuel Wallerstein, Wallerstein blends the approach of André Gunder Frank with the history of Fernand Braudel in his bid to examine what might be termed the prehistory of modern capitalism. Wallerstein's analysis of the modern world system is not yet completed but running through his works so far is an elaborate typology of global systems which takes the following form:

1. Small-scale, reciprocal mini systems;
2. large-scale world empires containing many different socio-political and ethnic groups united by an overarching and centralized political structure;
3. world economies which contain within their bounds many different units, but in contrast to world empires, without any political cohesion. In world economies the critical variable is the economic rather than the political connections.

Wallerstein up to now has concentrated upon investigating the modern world system, locating its origins in the fifteenth century. The growth of the late medieval and modern market and the ensuing worldwide division of labour in his opinion generated a basic distinction between core countries (Frank's metropolis) and peripheries (Frank's satellites). The two are linked by unequal exchange in which high-wage (but low supervision), high-profit, high-capital intensive goods produced in the core are exchanged for low-wage (but high-supervision), low-profit, low-capital intensive goods produced in the periphery.

Frank and Wallerstein's major achievement has been to bring sophisticated analyses of capitalist evolution and global inter-connections to bear on the critical issues of modernization in Third World countries. Their history may be readily chal-lenged as gross oversimplifications, but their fundamental approach in which the relations of global space are a major criteria is undeniably beyond dismissal. Wallerstein's work, in particular, has influenced Smith's formulation of regional production-distribution networks.

Dependency theory, however, is in more difficult territory where commodity production was absent or highly restricted. Wallerstein's mini-systems require closer definition, as several prehistorians have noted (Renfrew & Cherry, 1986). Local events cannot be attributed straightforwardly to the domi-nance of inter-regional connection by an exploitative trade partner. Regions have always formed their own personalities which in turn affected the short-lived configurations of those inter-regional linkages. Carol Smith in a historical account of Guatemala, makes this point (1984). She maintains that there will be a dialectical relationship between global systems and regions, and for what might be best described as historical reasons local forces may as readily distort a greater socio-economic trajectory as conform to it. In short, she points out that the expansion of capitalism in Guatemala, a peripheral region of a world system may be strongly influenced by local (historical) responses and cultural resistance (Smith, 1984: 224–25). As Eric R. Wolf notes the great powers and the Third World share the same historical trajectory. Very often, though, the latter are obscured from view up until the recent age of the anthropologist. Even then, colonialism may have obscured the knowledge of the pre-colonial past which is necessary to comprehend the mechanics of global economics. Spatial data recovered as archaeology may enable us to provide temporal dynamism to the otherwise imperious dance of successive great states upon colonial terrain. History, Wolf intimates, is not how it often seems to westerners; it is still in need of documentation and very far from being understood.

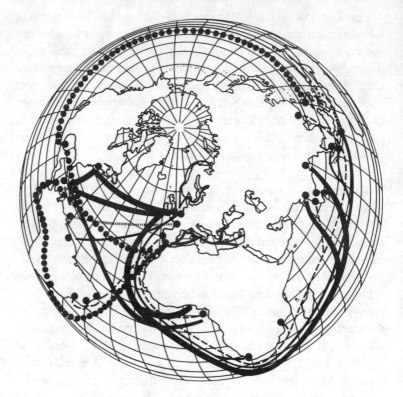

**Figure 3** *Braudel's summary of the 'octopus grip of European trade . . . to cover the whole world' in 1775. The routes shown simply indicate the major itineraries taken by all the ships of the various trading nations.*
*Source: Braudel, 1984.*

This is especially the case of market formation and accounts readily for the contentiousness of Dalton's work as well as the division between the substantivists and formalists on this issue.

Primitive and peasant markets necessarily amount to more than just bustling places. As institutions they express economic trajectories which underpin not only the past but the present as well. This book aims to examine a few pertinent issues about 'what markets are not' (to quote George Dalton), about the origins and development of markets as well as their political implications. Those who figured in market history as well as those influenced by these institutions will also be considered. In addition, the place of money in the evolution and development of market-places will be discussed. These themes amount to only a few of those many on this topic which deserve scrutiny.

## 2

# Markets in partially commercialized economies

Markets, most scholars would concur, are important components of the high-energy infrastructure essential to stratified social systems. Similarly, some measure of agreement exists with Carol A. Smith (1976a: 310) that stratification in agrarian or peasant societies depends upon:

1. differential access to and control over the means of exchange;
2. the types of exchange between producers and non producers as they affect and are affected by the spatial distribution of the elite, and the level of commercialization in the region and beyond.

Markets, then are integral mechanisms of the political economy in pre- and early state societies. As might be expected, however the inception of the market-place itself is a subject of much debate. How is it introduced into those societies in which reciprocity involving gift exchange is the dominant mode of exchange? I intend in this chapter to discuss the 'prehistory' of competitive markets. In particular, I shall attempt to describe the features of partially commercialised systems, including dendritic and solar-place systems. It is my contention, based upon European historical evidence summarised in the latter part of the essay, that competitive markets develop from deeply embedded socio-economic roots. In many cases, as I hope to illustrate, primate markets are the forerunners of the peasant marketing systems familiar from recent history as well as modern times.

The pre-market economics of aboriginal societies, as count-less economic anthropologists have illustrated, are far from simple. These are systems in which (to use Smith's terminology) the power of the elite is thoroughly constrained by social regulations; where gift exchange is the principal economic transaction because commodity production does not exist. In such systems the domestic mode of production, focussed upon kin relations is pre-eminent. Production in these societies, as a rule, is low, and mostly meets the needs and requirements of the community. Surpluses, if they occur, are usually employed as reserves for the community (in times of conflict or famine), and in sumptuary rites. Nevertheless, the populations of pre-market societies can be large. The Trobriand Islands, for example, maintained large communities when Malinowski carried out his fieldwork during the period of the Great War. Likewise, it may come as a surprise, for example, to discover that the populations of post-Roman states in Western Europe were broadly similar to those of Neolithic times, although the two worlds differed enormously in other respects. Population, therefore, provides an important pro-ductive variable in these circumstances but it does not necess-arily determine economic development (cf. Cowgill, 1975).

Trade appears to take two rather different forms in such societies, each with implications for the evolution of market systems. Most anthropologists are agreed that trade begins to satisfy social, political and ideological needs beyond basic subsistence. Trade is employed in 'social production' (Rathje, 1978) or 'social reproduction' (Godelier, 1977; Friedman and Rowlands, 1978). It takes the form of the objectification of labour in basically non-economic forms (that is in forms unrelated to the domestic mode of production) with explicitly social and ideological significance. Prestige-goods are obtained occasionally from within the system, but most often from out-side it. These are primitive valuables which are manipulated in two basic modes of social production: the first limits access to strategic goods, while the second functions through their circulation.

The first mode is a withdrawal system in which the goal is to achieve credit or prestige by conspicuous displays of giving away goods and services invariably as gifts to the gods, while at the same time removing a sizeable proportion of the finite amount of goods and services from circulation so that any potential rival is prevented from contriving similar displays (cf. Gregory, 1980; 1982). This tends to be typical of many large social systems, and frequently involves the entire community in public withdrawal acts like building monumental religious structures such as Egyptian or Mayan pyramids or the lavish burying of dead leaders such as occurred in Iron Age and migration-period Europe. In the second mode the strategy involves the circulation of the primitive valuables obtained through trade. This dispersal system usually occurs in smaller social systems and involves individual sponsorship of reciprocal exchanges at shifting nodes in the system, with the consequent circulation of wealth throughout the society. The classic example of this mode is the 'big-man' system in parts of Melanesia. Wealth circulates in this system as do the socio-political positions it legitimizes. Goods are not withdrawn, but instead they continually circulate within the system, even providing competitors with a temporary taste of status as they process the valuables. The 'big man' system contrasts sharply with the material extravagance of the 'gifts to gods' mode. The lavish withdrawal of goods by destruction or feasting legitimizes the position of the elite responsible for administering the system, and simultaneously decreases the access to symbolic wealth of potential competitors, thereby establishing status through credit. The withdrawal system, however, is often predicated upon the existence of prestige goods connections, through which some of the sumptuary objects are obtained. Clearly, if the source of the goods and services dries up, the leadership will face a grave crisis of public confidence.

These two modes reflect contrasting political economies. The withdrawal system functions through ranked spheres of exchange with ascribed roles leading to centralized, often theocratic leadership. In the 'big man' system, by contrast, power is gained through the continual dispersal of goods. Hence among the Kaoka there is a saying that 'the giver of the feast takes the bones and the stale cakes; the meat and the fat go to the others' (Hogbin, 1964: 66). Both economic modes, however, function as a result of obtaining resources which can be socially manipulated. The acquisition of these prestige goods may come through a variety of forms. In aboriginal contexts a common mechanism is what Colin Renfrew has called 'down-the-line' trade: primitive valuables are passed from one group to the next over long distances, often in exchange at each stage for some item of reciprocal value. A well-known illustration of this form of long-distance exchange occurred in Queensland, where aboriginal bands linked to other bands exchanged spears for stone axes over a distance spanning approximately 400 miles south from Cape York (Sahlins, 1974: 281). Renfrew has postulated that similar chains existed in Europe and the Near East in the Neolithic to disperse prestige goods such as obsidian, amber and spondylus shells which have remarkably wide archaeological distributions (1975). The mechanism may also account for the widespread distribution of late classical east Mediterranean valuables such as silver dishes, coptic teapots and jewellery interred by migration-period communities in England, Gaul and Scandinavia, practizing the 'withdrawal' mode described above (Werner, 1961; Hodges, 1982: 31–9).

Trade goods, alternatively, are distributed through agents – either controlled merchants or middlemen operating as independent communities. The agents themselves will be considered more fully in later chapters, but some brief illustration of their role is appropriate at this point.

Merchants operating under controlled circumstances played a decisive role in the colonization of the Third World and the spread of capitalism. Countless ethnographic illustrations depict, for instance, European merchants exchanging manu-factured commodities for bulk 'raw materials' such as foodstuffs or labour (slaves). The commodities were employed by the primitive party to the commerce for manipulating the local political economy. (The implications of this unequal exchange are examined later in this chapter). Exchanges of this kind, however, are not simply a feature of Immanuel Wallerstein's world systems; Herodotus describes 'the silent trade' between Carthaginian merchant-adventurers and North African tribesmen which attests the prehistoric beginnings of trade between unequal parties:

The Carthaginians also tell us that they trade with a race of men who live in a part of Libya beyond the Pillars of Heracles. On reaching this country, they unload their goods, arrange them tidily along the beach, and then, returning to their boats, raise a smoke. Seeing the smoke, the natives come down to the beach, place on the ground a certain quantity of gold in exchange for the goods, and go off again to a distance. The Cathaginians then come ashore and take a look at the gold; and if they think it represents a fair price for their wares, they collect it and go away; if, on the other hand, it seems too little, they go back aboard and wait, and the natives come and add to the gold until they are satisfied. There is perfect honesty on both sides; the Carthaginians never touch the gold until it equals in value what they have offered for sale, and the natives never touch the goods until the gold has been taken away (Herodotus: 307)

Many prehistorians now account for the diffusion of ideas in middle and later prehistoric Europe through unequal trade partnerships of this variety (Frankenstein & Rowlands, 1978; Bradley, 1984; Renfrew & Cherry, 1986). Accordingly, it is not at all surprising that the Roman 'world empire' (to use Wallerstein's term) readily engaged in unequal trade relations of the kind envisaged here. Julius Caesar, for example, describes romanised merchants in the Gallic *oppidae* he was planning to sack. Plenty of archaeological evidence, ranging from coins to military equipment, convincingly attests the booming exchange of Roman manufactured commodities for bulk goods with tribes beyond the imperial frontiers in the first and second centuries A.D. (Eggers, 1952; Wheeler, 1954; Hedeager, 1979). Tacitus alludes to a Roman merchant venturing to the Orkneys. The Danish archaeologist, Klavs Randsborg, has shown the implications of Roman traders penetrating Danish Iron Age society (1982; 1985; forth-coming). Access to Roman goods altered Iron Age society and, in particular, its political machinery. Social reproduction necessarily came to depend upon the flow of primitive valuables. But when the flow of goods waned with the economic crises of the Roman Empire there was bound to be trouble in store for the chiefs whose status was related to gift-giving (in life and to the gods). Randsborg regards the Germanic raids of the late third century as a corollary to the previously peaceful acquisition of valuables via trade.

The role of 'middlemen' as opposed to merchants is in many respects more fascinating. Middlemen in this sense were essentially strategically-placed agents in pre-market conditions, while merchants were and continue to be the agents of market-based societies. The Phoenicians are the classic middlemen, operating widely around the Mediterranean at the dawn of European civilization. Likewise Frisian traders were catalysts in the development of early medieval trade around the North Sea. But just how these middlemen operated in worlds which were deeply suspicious of traders is now obscure. Just how obscure is reflected to some extent in the celebrated case of the Siassi Islanders. The Siassi islands lie virtually equidistant between New Britain and New Guinea in the Vitiaz Straits. The islands are poor in all manner of resources; virtually everything is imported. Yet the Siassi traders have been some of the richest people of their area. 'Their prosperity is the dividend of trade, amassed from a number of surrounding villages and islands, themselves better endowed by nature but tempted to commerce with the Siassi for reasons ranging from material to marital utility' (Sahlins, 1974: 282-84). The Siassi exchanged fish for root crops with the villages on Umboi Island; they were the point of sale of pottery, transhipping it from northern New Guinea. They claim, however, that the pots 'are the shells of deep water mussels. The Sios (of New Guinea) make a speciality of diving for these mussels and, after eating the flesh, sell the empty "shells" to the Siassi. The deception of it added to their value, was justified by the vital

part that pots have in overseas trade' (Harding, 1967: 139–40).
In the same way they controlled obsidian distribution from its
source in northern New Britain. 'But . . . equally important,
the Siassi constituted for their trade partners a rare or
exclusive source of bridewealth and prestige goods – such
items as carved pigs' tusks, dogs' teeth and wooden bowls. A
man in neighbouring areas of New Guinea, New Britain, or
Umboi could not take a wife without some trade beforehand
. . . with the Siassi' (Sahlins, 1974: 284). The Siassi were
integral in the maintenance of social production in each of the
regions with which they were connected. A similar role,
according to Geoffrey Irwin, was played until recently by the
potters of Mailu, part of the New Guinea islands, who
likewise manipulated extensive Melanesian trade connections
(Irwin, 1978). What the Siassi islanders and the Mailu potters
share in common is the ecological poverty of their home-base
which triggers – or at least appears to trigger – an
entrepreneurial spirit. The pattern may account for the
Frisians and the Gotlanders of medieval times: island farmer-
traders who amassed great wealth as they became axial forces,
commanding the distribution of prestige goods within the
North Sea and Baltic Sea respectively. The Hausa of West
Africa would seem to fall into the same category (Dalton,
1975).

However, the difference needs to be stressed between the
merchants operating out of market-based societies, and their
counterparts strategically placed in pre-market conditions.
The 'middlemen' were, in effect, expressions of regions,
whereas the merchants of Rome, of the caliphates, of the
Chinese dynasties or of the modern world system were agents
legitimized by their states. Middlemen broadly shared the
cultural and economic circumstances of those they served;
merchants, by contrast, were consciously manipulating the
imbalances distinguishing their home countries from those
with whom they were dealing. Put more boldly, middlemen
were involved in complex gift-exchange transactions; the
merchants, even the famed Genoese and Venetian traders of

the late Middle Ages, when exploiting social inequalities, were exchanging commodities for tribute raised through primitive social production in pre-state communities.

In all cases, nevertheless, trade had to be transacted somewhere. Even the 'silent' bartering of goods described by Herodotus occurred at a beach-site. Hence we approach the question of 'markets': places where an economic spirit existed which was alien to the pre-eminent mechanisms operating in these societies. Prestige goods exchange, however, may be controlled or uncontrolled. It may be focussed at beaches or in the compound of a chief or headman, as it was for example in the kula ring; or it may occur in less ascribed contexts, between specified trade-partners, as it did amongst the 'big-men' situations served by the Siassi islanders (Harding, 1967: 166–7). Yet are these markets, and can the system be properly described as peripheral (in Bohannan and Dalton's terms) or partially commercialized (in Smith's terminology)? Many of the aboriginal illustrations – not least, those recorded by Malinowski in the kula ring – suggest ephemeral, extremely low-level economic transactions which served socially integrative purposes often of enormous magnitude. Sahlins provides a vivid example from the first encounter between James Cook and the Hawaiians.

On 20 January 1778, when the *Resolution* and *Discovery* made their initial anchorage at Waimea, Kaua'i, a satisfactory traffic began almost instantaneously between the British and ordinary Hawaiians, both on shore and about the ships. The local people provided foodstuffs in return for iron goods, which they took avidly in any form or shape. The women in the canoes alongside were already making their famous and unmistakable overtures to the seamen, their intentions of gratifying us in all the pleasures the sex can give (King Log: 20 Jan. 1778) (Sahlins, 1985: 136)

The encounter induced violations of sacred prohibitions by the women, it engendered widescale alterations to the cultural consciousness of the Hawaiian peoples, and it induced the native elite significantly to develop their political economy to meet these new circumstances. Consequently, after this brief but phenomenal encounter, the chiefs felt it necessary to adopt the manners of Europeans, to distinguish themselves from commoners and consciously appropriated the names of the European celebrities to enact altered sumptuary rites. The famous Kamehamelia, who conquered the islands between 1795 and 1810, apparently aspired to live like King George, and by the early 19th century, Hawaiian chiefs possessed such names as Billy Pitt, George Washington and Billy Cobbet (Sahlins, 1985: 140–1). Yet despite the inescapable significance of the exchange (in material and information), it was hardly a market transaction. Like all early prestige goods encounters, a 'sale' and some kind of limited bargaining occurred, but the situation lacked 'a symmetrical and inverse competition among buyers and among sellers' (Sahlins, 1974: 301). Competition and price regulations, two primary characteristics of market systems, were absent. But in these transactions we define the roots of the partially commercialized marketing to which Smith refers. This is most often focussed around central places, and occurs at points in time when social production is sensitive and receptive to change.

*Gateway Communities and Partially Commercialized Economies*

In the history of market development the gateway community has a special place. This is the node in an inter-regional trading system where commercial activity for a number of reasons becomes concentrated. Research by archaeologists, able to chart the development of trade over long periods of time, indicates convincingly that gateway communities reflect the growing complexity of prestige goods exchange, and of political economies in general. These places, in fact, appear to be expressions of ascribed and centralized trade, mostly related to 'withdrawal' systems of wealth. Yet, to complicate matters, most gateway communities also became centres of aggregated production prefiguring an essential aspect of integrated market systems. Therefore, it is necessary to begin by defining the gateway community carefully, since sites of this kind are commonly treated in the anthropological and historical literature with an imprecision that has many political ramifications.

'Gateway community' is a term used by the geographer A. F. Brughardt (1971) and introduced to archaeology by Kenneth G. Hirth (1978). It has a more precise meaning than emporium, entrepôt and even the port-of-trade, first adopted by Karl Polanyi. (The confusions regarding port-of-trade will be described below). A gateway community exists at passage points into and out of a distinct natural or cultural region and links this region to external trade routes. It is in effect the monopolistic market featured in the dendritic central-place system described by Carol A. Smith (see chapter 1). Gateway communities tend to be located along natural corridors of communication, often at critical points between areas of high mineral, agricultural or craft productivity. (Gateway communities have existed at the mouths of the Rhine and Rhone valleys, for instance, at several points in later prehistoric and early historic times.) The primary function of these settlements, it is generally believed, is to satisfy the demand for traded goods.

The origins and development of gateway communities have barely been examined by historians because they often lie in the misty depths of ethnohistory. European studies, however, indicate roots in prestige goods exchange systems rather than as a response to the settling of sparsely populated frontier areas (as Hirth (1978: 37) suggests). The late Iron Age emporia of Britain, places like Hengisbury Head and Camulodunum, appear to have begun as passage points, where the exchange of prestige imports was controlled. Roman or Gallic merchants apparently brought wine in amphorae, fine metalwork and other promotional materials which were exchanged for native resources such as slaves, minerals and the like. Control of the trade, in the first instance, appears to have been a critical variable in the feasting which not only sustained tribal ranking but also proved to be an integrating device of essential social importance to the configurations of late Iron Age politics (Hazelgrove, 1982).

Similarly, Early Anglo-Saxon 'kings' appear to have created neutral landing places as points where alien merchants and selective natives might engage in administered exchange. Excavations at Ipswich (Suffolk) have brought to light traces of such activities relating to trade between the Wuffingas dynasty of East Anglia and the Merovingian court of Austrasia in the Rhineland. Through this place doubtless came the fine jewellery and other prestige objects buried in the great seventh-century tomb at Sutton Hoo – a classic expression of the withdrawal system described in the earlier part of this chapter (Hodges, 1988a).

Simple fairground-like gateway communities like Ipswich commonly prefigure the construction of more urban variants; this simple type, therefore has been termed type A (Hodges, 1982a; 1982b). The formation of type A sites, it should be remembered represent a significant political and economic shift from those times when aliens journeyed to Anglo-Saxon courts and elite residences inland. The frontier position of the settlements reflects the growing importance of imported goods in Anglo-Saxon society. Hence the elite were necessarily concerned to prevent lower-ranking competitors from within their tribe interceding in the exchange – a danger which to some extent bears out Dowling's point discussed in Chapter 1, that within limits competition, and the concept of infinite needs does exist before the inception of price-regulated markets (cf. pp. 14–15). Not surprisingly, in the Anglo-Saxon case, the inception of type A gateway communities coincides with inflation (in the first three decades of the 7th century) in the destruction of goods in a highly conspicuous burial rite.

The type A sites must in many ways have resembled the temporary character of later medieval Icelandic fairs. According to Porlaksson, merchants came to trade at Gasar, Eyrar and Hvitarvellir between June and September. Local

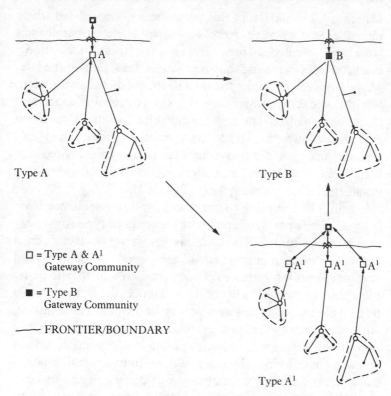

**Figure 4** *A typology of gateway communities. Type A, a disembarkation point and trading-place, may give rise to either type A¹, multiple/competitive gateway communities, or type B a primate centre concerned with production as well as distribution.*
*Source: author.*

chieftains administered the trade, set prices and took steps to prevent competition. The occasion also offered the chieftains the opportunity to interact with their rivals, to resolve disputes and to discuss legislative matters (Porlaksson, 1978). These were occasions, perhaps, for some specialist craftsmen to set up shop and trade their wares. But on the whole such communities were peripheral to the region in terms of production. Type A gateway communities, therefore, are peripheral markets in the sense described by Bohannan and

Dalton (see chapter 1). In this sense these places existed where market-places as such were absent and the principle was weakly represented. In many respects, too, these were periodic markets, foreshadowing the great saint's days' fairs of the later Middle Ages. Yet unlike the fairs of the medieval and modern worlds, type A gateway communities were probably dependent upon personalized trading partnerships. Limited medieval evidence shows that trade partnerships underpinned this system, just as it did in recent Melanesian cases, where the history of trade was dependent upon the individuals in organizing it (cf. Sahlins, 1974: 298–301).

It would be tempting to chart an inexorable sequence from prestige goods partnership through a series of type A gateway communities to fully fledged market systems. But such a sequence, while it may exist, glosses over the political and economic hurdles, rather as if one considered history to be no more than rattling off a list of dates. Hence, the formation of a neutral frontier site marks a new step in the political economy; an even greater step occurs with the creation of densely populated, permanent or semi-permanent emporia, type B gateway communities (Hodges, 1982a). In most smaller political systems only one community will be found, but in large polities encompassing several loosely bound territories or regions there are likely to be several emporia of this type.

Type B communities are conspicuously primate centres in the rank-size sense, often being many times larger than any other regional settlements. On the one hand, type B emporia obviously relate to the increasing scale of commerce, but as significantly, such sites mark the intentional development of controlled regional production concentrated alongside the traders. Superficially, of course, this type of community resembles a colony - a trading settlement imposed upon an alien territory. In practice, however, colonies such as those belonging to the Greeks in later prehistory, or to the British in modern times were administered by the traders or at least, alien administrators. These were explicitly alien mechanisms imprinted upon primitive economies, principally to acquire bulk commodities such as cereals, furs, slaves and so on.

The type B gateway community owes its origins to rather different conditions. First, it appears to be a response to the opportunities offered through trade connections with an alien territory. Maximizing trade, in other words, seems to have been the goal. In this respect we are witnessing the impression made by a pristine state on a receptive secondary one. Yet the early medieval examples do not indicate any great changes in the type of commodity exchange: as in the stage A communities, goods are of a luxury kind, principally for use in maintaining social integration within increasingly segregated ranked spheres of exchange. However, conspicuously, native crafts were developed alongside those of the alien communities.

Two splendid illustrations of this ambitious redirection of the political economy are Hamwih, Middle Saxon Southampton and Hedeby or Haithabu, now in West Germany but originally a Danish emporium. Hamwih was the emporium of the highly centralized West Saxon kingship. A small type A settlement may have existed here in the earlier seventh century, but about AD 690 the low-lying ground by the river Itchen was dramatically developed. In an age (lacking towns) when great monasteries covered perhaps an area of a hectare and accommodated no more than a hundred persons, Hamwih was laid out over some 40 hectares and must have had a permanent population of as many as 5000. (The West Saxon kingdom must have had a population in the order of 100,000-250,000 (cf. Hodges, 1988a).) The scale of the achievement within the political and demographic parameters of the age is conspicuous enough. But it is clear from the grid of streets lined with buildings that the intention was an explicit one. A great central street, some 14 metres wide cannot by coincidence have resembled the *agora* of classical times and prefigured the *Einstrassenanlage* of the Middle Ages: it was a conscious attempt, using thousands of tons of gravel, to replicate a concept seen elsewhere. Equally tons of manufacturing rubbish, mostly deposited in disused storage pits, betrays the principle function of this place.

The combination of evidence implies that a West Saxon king, probably Ina (690-722), consciously constructed a

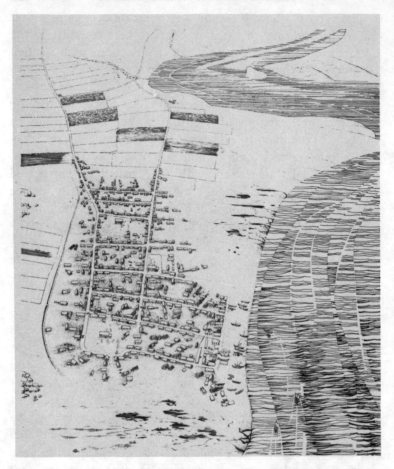

**Figure 5**   *A reconstruction of Hamwih or Hamwic, Middle Saxon Southampton beside the River Itchen. The illustration provides an artist's impression of the grid of streets, including the wide 'high' street running down the right-hand side of the settlement. The line of the boundary ditch can also be made out on the far left-hand side. Illustration reproduced courtesy of Southampton City Museums.*

market – even to the point of imitating the classical *agorae*, still to be seen, if often overgrown with weeds, in parts of Britain, Gaul and of course, Italy. However, in this unstable political climate the king evidently endeavoured to control not only the flow of imports, but also the regional production and distribution of native crafts. Indeed, unlike later medieval towns with their prominent tenemental divisions, Hamwih possessed no internal fences or ditches. Only a deep outer ditch, symbolically distinguishing it from the rest of Wessex bears any resemblance to a property boundary. (In this it resembles Anglo-Saxon palaces which comprised an assemblage of building enclosed within a ditch rather than the normal villages of the time in which each farm was located within a fence.) The implication is that whatever happened within its bounds was separate, different and monitored by the king's reeves. Outside it, the domestic mode of production entered its twilight (Hodges, 1988a). The Church had begun to transform attitudes to production, leading the shift from a world of gift-giving towards commodity production based upon landed property. Clearly, the inception of Hamwih marks an important step in the development of the West Saxon political economy.

Hedeby or Haithabu is an analogous case in some but not all respects. This site lay at the base of Denmark, on its frontier in the late eighth and ninth centuries with the Carolingian Empire. Significantly, it also lay astride a riverine route that connected the North Sea with the Baltic. The earliest emporium, known as the South Settlement, was a small village of unimposing form. However, like Hamwih, a new town was suddenly planned and laid out at Hedeby with dwelling/work-shops located within a grid plan of streets. Hedeby almost certainly evolved as an entrepôt managed by the Danes to which traders from the Carolingian, Scandinavian and Slavic - territories came. The hand of a controlling authority is apparent when the preceding, small amorphous community to the south is compared with the designed market, dated accurately by dendrochronology to the 810's. As at Hamwih, local craftsmen gathered and produced a wide range of materials, serving southern Jutland. But Hedeby notably differed from Hamwih as its aim was to be an entrepôt, through which the highly competitive and unstable Danish elite could acquire goods in an evidently escalating system of conspicuous consumption

(Randsborg, 1980). Moreover Hedeby was one of several emporia given life by the great arcing series of trade networks linking the Carolingian Empire in the West via the Baltic Sea through western Russia to the Abbasid Caliphate in the Orient. It was, therefore, very much a trading settlement which took advantage of a embryonic world trading system.

Hedeby's position as an entrepôt makes it closer in function to the Frisian emporia of this period. Dorestad is the most famous of these, but others are attested at Domburg, Walcharen and Medemblik. These were communities occupying a high risk landscape on the margins of the Continent which achieved extravagant wealth as middlemen by taking Carolingian commodities to northern Frisia and Denmark, and returning with Scandinavian products (as well as silver that originated in the Orient) (Hodges and Whitehouse, 1983). Like Hamwih and Hedeby, these settlements were a response to the opportunities not only to maximize trade, but also to develop local production. Emporia of this kind, in fact typify the vicissitudinous period of chiefly connections pre-dating the inception of nation states in tenth-century Europe. Many were much smaller than Hamwih, reflecting limited political authority perhaps, as well as the restricted productive capacities of their territories. But all indicate the drive to bring together a range of economic facilities at one point for political purposes.

The rationale for these achievements may have been as transient as Cook's discovery of Hawaii, and it is important to note that no early medieval king was able to inaugurate a dynasty as a result of creating and running an emporium. Yet the type B emporia mark a new direction in the political economy. Notably, a dual economy evolves. As Carol Smith has noted, the region immediately surrounding the monopolistic central-place assumes some of the economic and cultural character percolating from the emporium, in sharp contrast to the low-order settlements in the wider parts of the region. Attitudes to production in the sub-region nearest the emporium, as well as cultural promotion become increasingly competitive, and potentially divisive. Yet in those territories where the management of society was effective, to overcome potential spatial divisions, it is likely that attitudes to production might change and with this attitudes to resources.

Consequently, the type B emporia necessarily reflect a critical stage in the development of political economy. To a large extent influenced by widescale connections, these places became a preparatory to the economic take-off required to generate price-regulated market systems. But it is important to stress that the controlled type B gateway community, unlike the colony, was concerned with prestige goods as much as regional production. Either the demise of the prestige goods system or (since this is a chicken-and-egg situation) changes in the status of kingship with consequent increased emphasis being placed on commodity rather than gift production, may have altered their attitudes to resource management. In either case the rationale for the gateway community was no more. Too often historians (and archaeologists in their wake) assume that emporia simply gave way to competitive markets, without appreciating the very different political and economic mechanisms underpinning these institutions. In decline, however, some gateway communities evidently adopted a new role. Hirth proposes several possible paths for a gateway community in these circumstances:

1. The gateway community will lose portions of its original hinterland and will undergo an economic decline regressing to a level concomitant with that of its new competitors.
2. It will undergo slight economic decline but will retain some control over its former hinterland.
3. There may be an intensification of economic interaction within unaffected portions of its hinterland and new areas may be brought under the gateway's control.
4. It may force a shift in its major emphasis from the control of interregional trade to the tighter integration of economic activity within its own physiographic

region. There would be an increase in central place activities to ensure the survival of the existing social organization.

5. It may evoke more complex forms of sociopolitical authority with which to combat increased economic competition (Hirth, 1978: 42).

Each response, of course, depends upon historical context. James Doran's computer simulation of these circumstances (1979), like the oversimplified cultural trajectories postulated by ecological anthropologists, highlight the outlines of change only and make no sense of the complex social permutations involved. Similarly historians have yet to grapple with the political implications of these sites. Their formation, the mechanisms for maintaining them and eschewing periodic inflation, and their demise, like the precarious balance of restrictive commodity production alongside kin-motivated gift exchange are historical aspects of many proto-state societies that warrant greater attention.

## Ports-of-trade

Polanyi's concept of the port-of-trade is still commonly used and, therefore, merits consideration in this context. Polanyi regarded this as a site offering security to the foreign trader, with facilities for anchorage, disembarcation, storage and where an agreement existed upon the goods to be traded, the benefit of judicial authorities. Polanyi also defined the port of trade as a neutrality device, 'a derivative of silent trade . . . and of the neutralized coastal town (1963: 30). In fact, in his general essay on this institution he included places as diverse as early medieval Dorestad and Hedeby and the eighteenth century slave port of Whydah in Dahomey, West Africa. In most cases his examples have been challenged as lacking the precision necessary to sustain the concept (Hodges, 1978). Nevertheless, the American archaeologists, William L. Rathje and Jeremy Sabloff (1973) proposed a well-considered bundle of criteria in order to define this institution more precisely. Their criteria were as follows: a port-of-trade should:

1. be at a transition zone;
2. be a small political unit;
3. have a large population;
4. be little concerned with retail distribution within the port's surrounding area.

Rathje and Sabloff proposed Cozumel, a corralline island 16 km off the northeastern coast of the Yucatan peninsula, as a port-of-trade, because it adequately met these criteria. Subsequently, however, they withdrew the proposal when fieldwork and historical research revealed its similarity to a chain of other late Mayan monopolistic centres (Freidel and Sabloff, 1984). Cozumel, in fact, resembles the short-lived emporia around the North Sea/Baltic Sea zone of Carolingian and early Viking times (see above). As Rathje and Sabloff discovered, the criteria take insufficient account of the inter-regional context of the institution. George Dalton, however, has made a powerful case for Polanyi's model being 'a very flexible institution which exhibited several sorts of variation, some of which (the political and locational) he [Polanyi] himself described' (1978: 102). In his analytical treatment of this issue Dalton argues that Polanyi and his associates tried to do three things:

1. They tried to specify the core attributes of ports-of-trade in order to explain the rationale for their existence, the functions they performed, their political and economic organization and the constellation of circumstances that created them.
2. The Polanyi group also described variations among ports-of-trade in their organization, functions, and political and locational circumstances.
3. Above all, Polanyi and his associates contrasted such politically-administered trade with the historically

later and very familiar market trade, which not only came to dominate European and then worldwide international trade, but which also, in Polanyi's view, grew out of its very different port-of-trade origins in almost as vividly contrasting a way, one surmizes from Polanyi's emphasis, as the 'metamorphosis a butterfly undergoes in growing out of its very different origins as a caterpillar.' (Dalton, 1978: 102–03)

Dalton also emphasized that it was important to Polanyi to invent terms like port-of-trade because the English language contains only one conceptual vocabulary to analyze international trade, the vocabulary of conventional economics. Administered trade, the substantivists are eager to point out, cannot be summed up in the terminology of formal economics. As we have already argued (in chapter 1), there is much rationality in this belief. Nonetheless, Polanyi's rather sketchy concept, as Rathje and Sabloff discovered (and as Dalton acknowledges), covers a wider range of institutions and, consequently fails to specify its central theme clearly enough. Polanyi may be charged with over-emphasizing the spatial characteristics of the port-of-trade without full reference to the political economy of which it formed an important part. Hence, in his view, the port-of-trade is a device of political neutrality, yet in most of his illustrations it was designed and maintained by a political elite. Although he considers each of his examples as places where administered trade occurred, in Hedeby and Viking Age Birka (in Sweden) these were chiefly expressions of a complex kin-based mode of production (as was noted above), while Wydah in Dahomey functioned in a world system's commodity market, handling bulk goods – amongst others, slaves. The distinction between gateway communities and solar central-places operating in different economic spheres is more than a matter of splitting hairs; it is fundamental to the essential substantivist point that economic organization in aboriginal economies is socially controlled by polity, kinship, religion and the like, in sharp contrast to conditions where market exchange existed. For this reason it behoves the anthropologist and historian to consider the following variables when considering ports of trade and sites of superficially similar character:

1. composition and location of the participants in the commerce;
2. types of goods;
3. the inter-regional and regional motives for the exchange;
4. the nature of the local administration;
5. the settlement location.

As a result, it may be decided that the elaborated definition of Smith's typology (as used here) provides a more suitable framework for studying primitive markets in the terms first described by Polanyi.


*Solar central-places*

Carol A. Smith defines solar central-places as regional administrative centres with a low productive capacity and limited involvement in commerce. Such places command regions where the kin-based mode of production is dominant. As such these are political or spiritual centres not market-places. These are not strictly centres of production or distribution, and consequently price regulation is largely inappropriate to their operations. Yet in many cases local market exchange is kindled at these places. For this reason we need to examine how such places form, how they are maintained, and why in many cultures these have been the initial points for market exchange?

Solar central-places may often be traced back to social production in ranked societies. Power in such societies tends to have been focussed not only upon the destruction of wealth, but also on complementary withdrawal mechanisms such as building great monuments as a means of integrating society. The great conspicuous consumption centres of Mesoamerica, such as Teotihuacan and Tikal are stupendous examples of this phenomenon. The sprawling palaces of Minoan Crete, the Iron Age zimbabwes of central southern Africa and the monasteries of early Medieval Europe all belong to the same category. Chiefly status was ascribed and reinforced through capital accumulations and complex redistribution at these central nodes, while substantial resources were actually withdrawn for community status reinforcement. Archaeology once again charts the spatial growth of each institution. Many of these centres started as small shrines or sanctuaries which at some point in time were dramatically enlarged. The lifespan of the great Mesoamerican temple-cities was short; so too was the zenith of the Mycenean-Minoan palaces. Likewise the apotheosis of the zimbabwe and the early medieval monastery belongs to a brief phase when political resource strategies were especially volatile. These places could be used to embody the essential ideological elements of their societies. In particular, an ideology might be propagated to deny conflicts in society; similarly the ruling group might project its sectional interests as the universal interests of society; such places also tend to embody the naturalization of the prevailing relations within the system, making them appear immutable and fixed as if they embody natural laws. Hence, wealth in the form of tribute, gifts and labour is accumulated at these places, giving further status to those who control the place. Hence in their administrative capacity solar central-places command great resources, but these, as a rule are inefficiently used. Cultural levelling mechanisms, as Timothy Earle (1977) has demonstrated, tend to prevent the elite from articulating either the accumulated wealth or the ideological status in long-term political strategies.

The Carolingian monasteries of Western Europe are a good illustration of this point. These were consciously used by Charles the Great (771–814) as a means of welding his great empire together. Lacking an army sufficient to police a polity stretching from Bavaria to the Pyrenees, from Denmark to central Italy, Charles opted to use a spiritual mechanism to achieve the same end. He gave lands and exemption from tribute to certain strategically-placed monasteries, encouraged the redefinition of the monastic (Benedictine) code at several great councils to suit these needs and led the way in promoting a cultural renaissance. Small frontier monasteries like San Vincenzo al Volturno and Monte Cassino in central Italy were aggrandized, much as the type A emporia were replaced by the type B variant. At San Vincenzo a large planned monastery has been discovered, highly reminiscent of the descriptions of many other great ecclesiastical houses of this period. The monastery is notable for its projection of the new spiritual code, not only in its art but also in the highly-segregated lay-out of the place. It was splendidly decorated with re-used Roman materials as well as with paintings that consciously copied those of the classical period. Great store was placed on a grand new abbey church which attracted a large community of monks to the place. Yet at the same time the modular arrange-ment of the settlement meant that the monks were cocooned from visitors, and ordinary pilgrims were kept apart from the palatial quarters allocated to members of the elite. By conforming in these ways to the renaissance, San Vincenzo enjoyed brief prosperity as the Empire flourished. Patronage permitted a second phase of rebuilding in which these ideals were incorporated and expressed more powerfully. Then the Empire collapsed. With this San Vincenzo's patronage faded, and it was compelled to look to its own resources to sustain an unnaturally large population as well as a redundant ideology and like many monasteries, promoted regional development through the creation of surplus (Hodges, 1988b).

But was San Vincenzo ever a market? A nineteenth-century fair at the site may have origins in antiquity, but the connection is strictly hypothetical. We can only speculate in its case that it used its surplus labour and skills after the construction of the Carolingian monastery to produce for a regional market. Periodic markets in Carolingian times are, after all, only mentioned outside monasteries like Corvey and Verdun. Contemporary accounts show that abbots, like the imperial family, were aware of the merits of production; certainly some acquired rights to trade through the emporia. For this reason later medieval markets developed around these shrines (see chapter 3). But as Renfrew showed in the case of the Minoan palaces, the primary function of the administration was to maintain resources sufficient to meet the ideological requirements (Renfrew, 1972; 1975). Moreover, Vincas Steponaitis in his study of the great sumptuary mounds of the Mississippi, argues that solar central-places of this kind were not developed at those places where the exploitation of subsistence could be most advantageously undertaken, but where the social environment could be manipulated most efficiently (Steponaitis, 1978). He argued that in complex and centralized ranked societies a relative measure of the degree of power wielded by the central authorities is the amount of tribute that can be exacted. Steponaitis, in other words, challenges the maximizing models of von Thunen as being appropriate in pre-market contexts where the factors of primitive tributary relations need necessarily to be taken into account. Social factors determined site location and, when the economy altered, the abandonment or isolation of economically inefficient locations.

The evidence for the market functions of such places remains highly ephemeral. Occasionally the collapse of the over-arching system, often of an inter-regional nature, generates the conditions for an alternative resource strategy as was noted in the case of medieval monasteries; more frequently as the great archaeological literature on ritual attests, systems of such complexity disappeared in divisive political upheavals. However, another variant of the solar central-place which merits a mention at this point is the emporium of the gateway community type B which with the collapse of its international connections (and prestige goods) is either forced into a swift phase of decline or (as Hirth anticipates: see above, p. 51) is adapted by the elite in the moment of political crisis to a more administrative function. Sites of this kind, with their origins in production and distribution rather than ritual, or spiritual, will be discussed in the next chapter.

## Peripheral market-places and the beginnings of market systems

So far I have considered administered or controlled centres where some marketing may have occurred while the primitive economy as a whole remained largely structured through the kin mode of production. The two classes of gateway community, and the low-level market exchange focussed upon sumptuary centres appear to have been related to political strategies invariably generated by exogenous influences and opportunities. Hence, it may be argued, trade and differential access to local resources may account for the peripheral markets in dendritic and solar central-place systems respectively. However, what happens if the spatial distribution of the elite takes a different form? In other words, if stratification is less pronounced does it follow that there are no incentives to market exchange?

The answers to these questions remain in the hands of anthropologists. Here we must return to the aboriginal context of economic dispersal. The circulating status and the practice of redistribution by 'big men' in particular, functions through competitive feasts like the banquets described in the Anglo-Saxon poem Beowulf. These are concurrently images of conspicuous consumption and the dispersal of wealth. Perhaps the most famous of all such occasions was the potlatch of the north-west American tribes. The destructive potlatch of the Kwakiutl of Vancouver and northern California was made famous by Franz Boas and later by Ruth Benedict: they recalled the frenzied, ritualistic destruction of blankets, boxes of fish oil and even on one occasion, a house, by a host chief trying to generate esteem through such a display.

Most anthropologists are convinced, however, that this conspicuous destruction witnessed late in the nineteenth century was a response to European trade, as competition between the various components of the Kwakiutl community reached a new pitch (Wolf, 1982: 192-94). Previously the rivalrous feasts had been less wasteful, with many visitors carrying back home some of the goods which were neither destroyed nor consumed in the great meals. Marvin Harris, for example, has emphasized the important ecological and economic advantages. First, the rivalry generated increased production in the component territories participating in the potlatch system. Secondly, rivalrous intervillage redistribution may have been ecologically adaptive as a means of overcoming the effects of localized, naturally induced production failures. Failures of the salmon run, for instance, might be met by attending the potlatch and carrying back vital supplies made available by the host chief. The tally was redeemed, of course, when the guests turned hosts and sought to become prestige creditors rather than debtors. A third factor arose from the continued failure of some groups. They were naturally attracted to those whose displays were most conspicuous, leading to population shifts which became more pronounced once European diseases and warfare penetrated the system. Increased population meant a larger labour force which gave rise to greater means for generating materials for the potlatch.

The potlatch redistribution, therefore, was embedded in the political economy, and in some respects is an example of ecological adaptation (Harris, 1980: 236-7). But no prices regulated the exchange between the peoples, let alone the chiefs. The concept of competitive buyers and sellers simply did not exist, although maximization for the system and rivalry between trade partnerships did. It compels us to conclude that the potlatch was a mechanism of the kin mode of production until the inroads of western capitalism became too great to disregard. Only then, as the anthropologists arrived, did the values change. The competition became greater and more militant, while goods like firearms began to assume precise values. The feast-places then began to resemble periodic market places. The circumstances are not so different from Anglo-Saxon England or Brahmin Thailand (Wheatley, 1975). Connections with a wider world in each case altered their world picture: these ultimately percolated through society, often leaving the elite practising redundant sumptuary rites for the sake of historical tradition (to the dismay of modern analysts). When the elite were in the position to abandon these sites, and to exercise full control over each level of exchange we witness the emergence of the competitive market. The transition involves mighty changes to all aspects of society, as the Kwakiutl experience rather tragically illustrates.

# 3

# Competitive markets

Put simply, the competitive market embodies the principle of buying and selling. The principle eclipsed the ethos of the feast-places which typified exchange in more primitive circumstances. The merchant and the craftsman now came into their own. But this catch-all definition barely sums up the complexities of this kind of exchange. Peasant markets, like peasantries, have taken many forms in anthropology and history (Dalton, 1972; 1973; Wolf, 1966; 1972). In this chapter, therefore, I shall attempt to outline some of the many features of competitive markets. Following this, I shall examine how markets formed. The historical examples used to illustrate this are based upon various sources to provide a long-running, wide-angled panorama of processes involved.

In many peasant societies the market-place is an urban phenomenon where craftsmen are aggregated to manufacture the commodities which are a principal feature of competitive market systems. These places differ from partially commercialized market-places because prices regulate exchange in an explicit form. Markets, it might be argued, appear in those societies in which relations are determined by tribute rather than kinship. Accordingly, in broad terms the market-place is an expression of a population divided between surplus producers and surplus takers.

The ubiquity of the market principle may also be broadly equated to a level of political complexity in which coercion plays a major role. Coercion is a critical feature, installed and maintained by private armies – the apparatus of the state. This coercion is enforced as a rule either by a ruling elite holding sway over the population or a collection of competing families. In either case control of markets is of the utmost importance for raising the tribute to sustain the private armies on which these elites depend. Moreover, the liberties created by stimulating competition unleash economic connections which invariably bring the system within Wallerstein's world systems (see chapter 1). The stranger becomes familiar in competitive market systems, wherein price-making exchanges are noteworthy for the anonymity and impersonality of the process in contrast to the administered and personal exchange relations of pre-state economies. The inception of markets, therefore, is the hallmark of great social changes.

The competitive market is defined not only by its price-regulation but by the production and distribution of commodities. Fully commercialized systems appear to integrate rural specialization with urban specialization (though see chapter 5). Peasants now appear to be specialists competing with other peasants in the production of surplus crops. This is another distinction between fully competitive and partially commercialized systems. In theory, through the exercise of tributary relations, everyone is affected by the market principle. This, at least, is the formulation with which Adam Smith opened the third book of his *Wealth of Nations* and many take to be the essence of western capitalism. In Smith's opinion, 'the great commerce of every civilized society is that carried on between the inhabitants of the town and those of the country . . . We must not . . . imagine that the gain of the town is the loss of the country. The gains of both are mutual and reciprocal . . .' (quoted by Finley, 1985a: 191–2). Karl Marx, however, attacked Smith's thesis with character-istic force in *Das Capital*: 'The foundation of every division of labour which has attained a certain degree of development and has been brought about by the exchange of commodities, is the separation of town from country. One might well say that the whole economic history of society is summed up in this antithesis' (1976: 472). The substantial division between Adam Smith and Karl Marx is to some extent illuminated by a

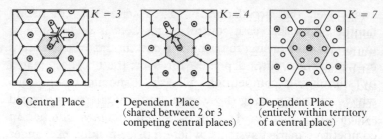

⊙ Central Place    • Dependent Place (shared between 2 or 3 competing central places)    ○ Dependent Place (entirely within territory of a central place)

**Figure 6** *Central place lattices based on the marketing principle (k=3), transport principle (k=4) and administrative principle (k=7).*
*Source: Haggett, 1965.*

century of anthropological and historical research which indicates the many forms of peasant markets. Each form, not unnaturally, is conditioned by particular (historical) social configurations. Let us begin, therefore, by examining some of these forms before considering the highly speculative question of how competitive market systems evolve in the first place.

The most familiar geographical expressions of market systems are those proposed by Walter Christaller (1966) (see chapter 1). Christaller defines an optimal, least-cost organizational structure within a network of regionally related sites. He believed that the sites in this network would adopt a hexagonal territorial tessellation of space which could be altered by moving the orientation of the hexagonal net, the magnitude of each territory, and the number and variety of sites served by each central place. His model depends upon two principles: (i) the population and (thus the) purchasing power are evenly distributed over an undifferentiated and unbounded surface, and (ii) maximization of profits and minimization of costs are regulated through the structured market system. The result is what Carol A. Smith terms interlocking central-place systems (1976a: 315). These systems, she argues, display both hierarchical arrangements and the linkages within the networks (see Fig. 1e & 1f) are broadly open to a wide range of relationships among all the places (and thus the people) in the system.

Christaller identified three essentially different properties within his model: the marketing, transport and the administrative principles. First, the marketing principle determines a settlement system in which distance between market-places and participants is minimized. The result is the densest settlement hierarchy of the patterns he considers. Christaller called this a $k=3$ pattern, where the $k$ value represents the total number of settlements served by the central place. In this pattern the value is made up of the central-place itself plus a one-third share in each of the six border settlements. As Fig. 6 shows, this one-third proportion is because each dependent place is shared between three central places (Haggett, 1965: 118–19). In sum, therefore, in this pattern higher order places share lower order places so that each higher order place is engaged with a total of 3 next lower order places (Fig. 6). Secondly, Christaller recognized the influence of transport as a means of creating a fluid central-place system wherein 'as many places as possible lie on one traffic route between two important towns. The more unimportant places may be left aside' (Christaller, 1966: 74). The hierarchy pattern resulting from the operation of the transport principle is identified as $k=4$. In this situation each higher place shares each next lower order place with one other higher order place; alternatively, half of each lower order place's activity is directed to one of two higher order places. Accordingly, those people in lower order places in this system are at an interactive disadvantage in comparison to their counterparts in a $k=3$ system. (The $k$-value relates to a pattern in which the hexagonal net around the central place has been turned through ninety degrees so that it possesses three half-shares in border settlements (Fig. 6).) Thirdly, the administrative principle leads to a settlement hierarchy in which each lower order place has only one higher order place. Here the constraint is that each higher order place exercises a monopoly over lower order places, sharing the interactions with no other place of similiar/equal order. This is a $k=7$ system wherein those in lower order market-places have much less choice for higher order market interaction than in either of the former two systems. (In this pattern the $k$ value is based upon the central place having control over six settlements (Fig. 6).)

Christaller's central-place theory, therefore, is not 'a behaviourial straightjacket' (Paynter, 1982: 140). Christaller was well aware of the complexities of spatial patterning and, simultaneously, the implications of multiple patterns occurring within one territory.

A major feature of the interlocking central-place model is that each market place is connected to one or more higher-level centres. This creates a network with several levels, several links between levels, and some hierarchically arranged administration of all the places in the system. G. W. Skinner, for example, in a seminal study of market structure in rural China, identified five tiers within the market structure. At the bottom exist minor or incipient markets. These are 'green vegetable markets' in which peasant produce is exchanged, and commodities are rarely traded. Next there are standard markets in which goods are exchanged within a defined market area. These are the starting point for the upward flow of agricultural goods and the terminal for the downward flow of imported commodities. Intermediate markets connect these standard markets to central markets which are strategically placed in the transportation network. Central markets are bulking centres where facilities for storage and wholesaling exist. At the apex of the hierarchy is the regional centre – a major administrative nexus for controlling the lower tiers. Skinner observes that each step up the hierarchy broadly involves an increase in the facilities and the range of goods available, as well as an increase in the size of the population (Skinner, 1976; 1964–5). In addition, to this hierarchically arranged dimension, some account must be taken of goods flowing to and from other regions. Interlocking market systems tend to lead to unbounded regions in which trade areas overlap. Supply and demand or price information is communicated across broad areas to ensure coordination of specialization. In particular, this allows for the specialization

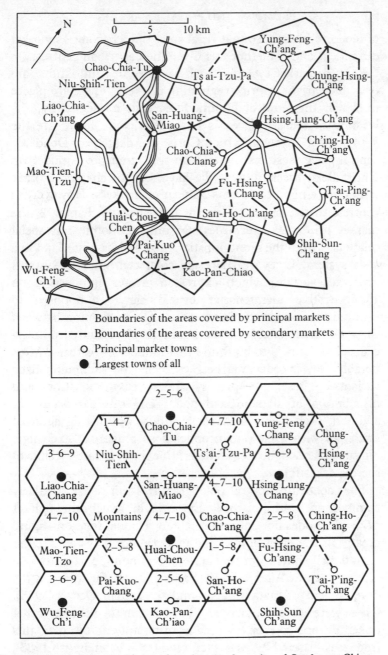

**Figure 7** *The distribution of markets in the region of Szechwan, China.*
*Source: Skinner, 1964-65.*

of food production, so that rural areas often become as market dependent and sometimes as diversified as urban centres.

Ranked market systems, such as those in rural China, are only one variant of price-regulating markets. There are places in which the flow of commodities and, consequently, the location of market-places is more restricted. There are the $k=4$ and $k=7$ systems which Christaller described. Dendritic central-place systems belong to the transport model in Christaller's thesis, but as we have seen in chapter 2 other issues are embodied in this pattern of markets. However, in contrast to the pre-state variant described in chapter 2, the market principle determines not only economic but social relations within the monopolistic centre and its hinterland in a $k=4$ system. Likewise there are solar central-place systems (the $k=7$ variant) which express a greater emphasis upon administrative maintenance over society as opposed to facilitating fluid economic relations. The distinction between these commercialized markets and their partially commercialized variants is to be found in a number of features. Most notably, lower-order markets exist in the commercialized variants. These are places where mass-replication and distribution of standardized goods and services occur. In addition, such places necessarily induce optimizing agrarian strategies with a view to producing surpluses for exchange. No such places or strategies determine the pre-state variants of these market forms.

The dendritic central-place ($k=4$) form is particularly common in world history. Emporia in which the market principle guides not only internal but regional relations figure greatly in the evolution of the modern world system. K. N. Chaudhuri shows, for example, that monopolistic trading centres such as Aden and Kilwa played a critical part in the development of marketing around the Indian Ocean (1985). These were entrepôts critically stationed on the sea-routes that linked Europe and Asia. In the late first millennium A.D. this trade was fostered by Arabs (cf. Hodges & Whitehouse 1983), but by the later Middle Ages, such was the wealth at stake, that

Western European states first intruded into the system then captured it. Hence, by the late sixteenth century, Aden, for example, while still independent, was subjected to an annual Portuguese naval patrol. In each case the international trade was rigorously controlled by the local governments, and only a fraction of the wealth trickled out to the regions in which each was situated. Archaeological surveys in East Africa in Kenya, Mozambique (Barker, 1978), Zimbabwe and on the island of Madagascar (Wright, 1983) show that very small amounts of the manufactured goods featured in the trans-oceanic trade was distributed from places like Kilwa and later, Zanzibar, and then occurred on Iron Age settlements.

Braudel and Wallerstein, similarly, have drawn attention to the role of monopolistic colonial ports in the development of the modern world system. The trading-places of the Hudson's Bay Company are good examples of such ports in the New World. In the controlled environments of these ports North American Indian goods were obtained for small numbers of manufactured articles. In the latter case, domination played an important part; but the Indian Ocean emporia, for example, were party to an extensive commercial system which was poorly rooted within the hinterlands of most of the ports involved. In both cases, markets form a linear arrangement rather than a pyramidal one of the kind associated with interlocking market systems. The linear arrangement is orientated towards a single point usually beyond the local agrarian system. In the chain leading to this centre there exist collecting points. But while many collecting places are connected with each other, they connect to only one price-setting market. This arrangement is not at all efficient for stimulating markets in the agrarian region (often it is quite the reverse), but is an efficient method for channelling the upward flow of raw materials (slaves, cash-crops, minerals, furs etc.) from the agrarian region and the downward flow of specialized goods from the monopolistic centre. However, as rural produce flows only intermittently between the lower-ranking markets, peasants cannot depend on the market for their food.

As a result they specialize in producing goods for a broad, often international market but largely depend upon their own subsistence produce supplemented by other less regular goods from that market chain (Smith, 1976a: 319-20). Such systems are a prominent feature of recent world history, and expressions of blatant exploitation.

Malacca, at the intersection between the Indian and Pacific Oceans, was one of the great emporia of the type under scrutiny here. In legend it was remembered as a pirates' haunt. By the early sixteenth century it swelled seasonally with traders who had crossed the two seas. Up to 84 languages were spoken, so it was said. Such diversity, which it shared with all the great emporia of this age, posed no threat. Rulers refrained from interfering in commercial affairs of the alien merchants, who in turn vouched for the good behaviour of their sailors. At Malacca locally appointed officers as well as those appointed by the trading parties ensured that well-oiled principles governed the collection of customs' duties as well as the process of buying and selling. These legal conventions were strictly enforced to the extent that Tome Pires, the Portuguese author of *Suma Oriental*, noted: 'Whoever is lord of Malacca has his hands on the throat of Venice' (Chauduri, 1985: 113).

A telling contrast to the largely independent emporia around the Indian Ocean is to be found in the colonial exploitation of the native Americans for furs. The fur trade first touched the food collectors and horticulturists of the eastern woodlands and subarctic. Dendritic central-places like New Amsterdam and the Hudson's Bay Station were positioned at the end of long collecting chains. Between the seventeenth and late nineteenth centuries the impact of this trade on the North Americans was considerable. European artefacts and cultural patterns drove a wedge through traditional native political configurations, altering them irrevocably. In particular, the pattern of social relationships held together by the exchange of American prestige goods was completely overtaken by the introduction of European manufactured articles. Inevitably

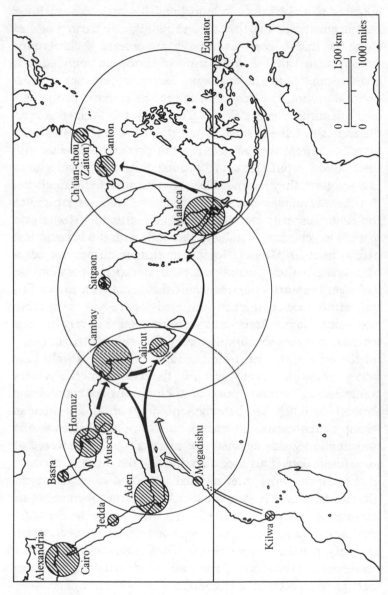

**Figure 8** *The structure of emporia trade in the Indian Ocean before 1500. Source: Chaudhuri, 1985.*

relations with the Europeans caused the old gift-exchange alliances to break down. Contagious illnesses like smallpox accompanied the arms, trinkets and manufactured commodities along the trade-routes. Eventually kin-ordered social groups were regulated by the circulation of European commodities, and in some cases the exchange led to the creation of new political groupings often affiliated to the emporia or markets in the dendritic chains. Tribes like the Huron, located around the shores of Lake Huron, found that they were strategically placed as intermediaries between the French to the East and the Iroquois populations further inland. As their involvement in trade grew, they lessened their commitment to horticulture. But their advantage was short-lived. The Iroquois aspired to the same prosperity and destroyed the Huron in 1648, largely in a bid to get a firmer stake in the trade with the French. But here as in other parts of North America, as European traders consolidated their economic and political position in nineteenth-century America, the balance between native fur-trapper/producer and European trader gave way to a grave imbalance. Native Americans were compelled to rely increasingly upon the lower-ranking markets/trading centres not only for the tools of the fur trade but for subsistence as well. Like peasant societies in many systems, the native Americans were compelled to commit more of their labour to maintaining themselves. They had become cash-croppers in a system in which entrepreneurs advanced both production goods and consumption goods against raw materials to be delivered at some future date. This specialization tied the native Americans into continent-wide, international networks of exchange, as producers in the predicament which Chayanov observed to be the peasant's lot (see chapter 2). In other words, the dendritic central-place system is a manifestation of the transformation imposed upon the native culture. The imbalance became more exaggerated as the scope of the emporia involved grew increasingly greater (Wolf, 1982: 158ff).

The difference between these two dendritic central-place systems amounts to more than a matter of semantics. Malacca was an autonomous emporium drawing upon a comparatively underdeveloped territory. New Amsterdam grew as an expression of the colonial exploitation of North-east America. The sultans of Malacca were drawing upon their own territorial resources as well as encouraging their merchants. The European emporia in the New World were dealing with alien territories. Once colonized and structured within a West European political system an interlocking competitive market system was forged in which, as Wolf puts it, the native Americans' lot was subsumed to greater, far more extensive economic targets.

In commercialized systems solar central-places are urban centres located in the middle of tributary hinterlands, all rural places being connected to this centre for their marketing. The ranking which otherwise distinguishes interlocking central-place systems is largely absent in this market variant. Hence, the solar central-place exists without competition from medium-sized places as intermediate centres. Lower order centres, however, tend to function for the exchange of vegetables and utensils. The market principle, therefore, exists, but is subordinated to the overarching political need to monopolize authority in one great place. Such places restrict competition and enable it to be closely scrutinized. Peasant producers, for example, are compelled to trade their produce in the monopolistic centre. The result is inefficient rural production, and equally inefficient distribution of commodities. Carol A. Smith has described several examples from modern Latin America. However, the later classical city, a subject which will be discussed further in this chapter, and the markets of the Abbasid Caliphate are also pertinent expressions of this type.

The caliph Al-Mansur is said to have laid the first brick of the great round city of Baghdad in AD 762, and within five years a huge city had been constructed by corvée labour. The settlement occupied about 500 hectares which was dominated by the caliph's palace, 200 metres long (Hodges & Whitehouse, 1983: 128). The place was chosen for its central location – a place where the rivers and roads of the orient met. The limited archaeology confirms the cosmopolitan character of its imports and attests to the productive capacity of its artisans. However, Robert Adams in his famous field survey of the lands beyond Baghdad reveals that under the Abbasids there was a significant depopulation of the Euphrates valley (Adams, 1981). As great wealth was accumulated in the round city, so the peasantry faced hardships unknown for nearly a millennium. One result of this centralization must be the periodic vulnerability of the Abbasid dynasty when its wider trading connections diminished. On one such occasion, in the early 9th century, a new central-place was constructed at Samarra – a city that was 35 kilometres long. As at Baghdad, the great palaces of the caliphate dominated the townscape while artisans adjusted to their new, hastily arranged circumstances (Hodges and Whitehouse, 1983: 151-6).

The peasant market, therefore, has taken many forms. First and foremost it must be viewed as a device for developing new social relations. At the same time the principles of supply and demand denote the removal of kin-based restrictions and the inception of widescale inter-regional interaction involving bulk trading. The market, therefore, is a feature of world empires and world systems, and in some respects often to be included in the apparatus of the state. But do states precede markets or are markets an instrument in the assertion of dynastic state control? In other words, how do partially commercialized market systems adopt the principle essential to tribute-based state societies?

### The Formation of Markets

The literature on the formation of markets is remarkably thin. This is perhaps not surprising, if the formation of markets is indeed part of a more general change which includes a political transformation, since the record itself will also be part of that change. In the first place it would continue to be

controlled, perhaps for a generation or more, by represen-
tatives of the older order with which the social liberties of the
market place are emphatically at odds, and will therefore lead
to silence on changes unwelcome to this order; the silence will
be broken only when the new order is in place, and ready to
record its own version of acceptable or legitimate history. For
example, Jacques Le Goff has demonstrated in his essay on
licit and illicit trades in medieval Europe (1980) that the
Church consciously opted not to write about market matters,
even though its members were actively involved in them.
Historians, therefore, have a real problem when it comes to
documenting economic change of this magnitude. Consequently, they like anthropologists and geographers have
tended to study modern circumstances and with reference to
*historical* descriptions in the prehistoric and early historic past
they have formulated models to explain the beginnings of
markets. As these historical descriptions may be justifiably
questioned, we are left to take note of the modern anthropological record.

Braudelian history will rarely be imitated but its thrust is
admired and to some extent trusted. The modern world
system is widely acknowledged to exist, and is no longer
regarded as a figment of neo-Marxist imagination. The present
North-South divide which threatens the Third World and
ultimately through their commercial and banking connections
with it the rich western communities, makes a point which has
seemed strangely less obvious, for example, to those studying
the Victorian Age (cf. Wolf, 1982). It is, therefore, an
inescapable fact that present (or even 20th-century) market
relations have been largely stimulated by the core-periphery
relations which, according to Wallerstein, are the essential
components of world systems (see chapter 1). The origins of
markets in Latin America like those in Central Africa cannot
be divorced from the impact of the present world and its
voracious capitalism (see Blomstrom & Hettne, 1985, for a
critique of these issues). An uncontroversial illustration of this
point can be found in Papua, New Guinea. C. A. Gregory

(1980) has shown how foreign churches, foreign states and foreign capital have been the agents of change. They introduced basic European institutions into Port Moresby and through a network of dendritic relations the interior communities were transformed from kin-based communities into minions of the great wheel of capitalism. New Guineans have become the cheap labour of new factories. At the same time markets strung out from Port Moresby into the highlands have effected an irrevocable economic change by bringing manufactured commodities to a hitherto isolated community. To afford these commodities, though, the Highlanders need cash, which they have to obtain through the factory work. The real thrust of Gregory's studies, however, has been to chart the persistence of traditional systems in the face of this market onslaught. The traditional ethics of kinship survive at the moment in a mutated form, reflecting the point made above that there will be attempts in the nexus of change to deny it. Hence, Gregory shows that in those areas outside the immediate control of foreign states and capital it is possible for paper money to change its social form and to function as an instrument of gift exchange in an increasingly archaic kin-based political structure (see also Gregory, 1982, for a fuller examination of this transition).

This New Guinea illustration is a small episode in the great European assimilation of the world. Unlike those episodes described by Eric Wolf in the United States, cited above, the New Guinean situation has yet to reach its final destiny. In another generation we may expect their kinship system to be mostly a memory and their fate to be in the hands of a world well beyond the rim of their world. Of course, it is not impossible - the way the world is proceeding - that New Guinea will be located in a core drawing upon peripheries from whence the island was once colonized!

So how can we ascertain the origins of market systems? The answer is hardly straightforward: a record is needed that documents all levels of society over a long period of development. This would make it possible to adjudicate between the two most familiar explanations of market formation which are:

1. The division of labour at a local and regional level generates the need for markets. Carol A. Smith calls those who adhere to this thesis the Adam Smith school. They hold that market trade is universal insofar as scarce goods are always allocated by some system in which supply and demand are brought into equilibrium by the relative values attached to goods of different scarcity (Smith, 1976b: 44). Market exchange will develop because natural differences in resource distribution creates scarcities that compel specialization and fully-fledged institutions of exchange. Population density is often seen as one triggering mechanism (cf. Smith, 1976b: 45), though discussing other circumstances George Cowgill (1975) has challenged the role of demographic density as an agent of social division.

2. Markets are initiated by long-distance trade contacts. Smith describes those who adhere to this thesis as members of the Polanyi school who 'consider market trade a rather "unnatural" human activity that requires certain specific conditions to develop forces exogenous to the domestic economy' (Smith, 1976b: 45). As we have seen, trade is compartmentalized to begin with at places where economic maximization will not threaten the social order. In Polanyi's view, true market economies, those permeated by the market principle, developed only once, when the economy took over society during the industrial revolution and capitalism emerged. It is a view not entirely endorsed by his students, of whom George Dalton, as we have seen, is perhaps the leader. Dalton holds that market economies pre-date industrialization and the great transformation.

These polarized views, as Smith shows, are in fact complementary. As she says 'Adam Smith's invisible hand generates the system, but Polanyi's sociopolitical variables provide the proper environment for the system to flourish' (1976b: 47). Many archaeologists have reached the same conclusion (e.g. Flannery, 1972; Wright and Johnson, 1975). Origins, in some senses, therefore, would appear no longer to be a problem – political centralization and commercial extension are aspects of the same process. That process, though, almost invariably begins with the creation of a primate centre and, in this respect, the division between the Adam Smith school and the substantivists might be respectively expressed as follows:

1. a transition from a primitive solar central-place system (see chapter 2) to competitive market-places in the region;
2. a transition from a primitive dendritic central-place system to competitive market-places, although the exact process might depend upon the constancy of the long-distance connections.

In short, the difference between the two schools rests on whether endogenous or exogenous forces transform the local social order.

It is not sufficient, however, to distinguish these differences in abstract terms. There is much to be learnt from observing the pattern of market formation over a long time period, and in adjacent though politically autonomous conditions. One of the most celebrated studies of market formation is Henri Pirenne's Princeton lectures entitled *Medieval Cities*. Countless anthropologists have been drawn to Pirenne's work or to that of his students and critics who have participated in the great and effervescent discussion of European town formation. Pirenne's thesis is today no more than a great shadow cast across European historiography (cf. Brown, 1974; Hodges & Whitehouse, 1983). In some respects his work has much in common with that of Bronislav Malinowski and Marcel Mauss (see chapter 1) insofar as he broke with a long tradition of research to emphasize the social and economic facets of the world he was studying. Before Pirenne most historians described the beginnings of medieval towns in essentially political or even legal terms. Pirenne brought the economic and social aspects into the foreground. It is not hard, incidentally, to account for his then radical thesis. Up until the First World War he was one of a number of historians trying to break with the emphasis upon constitutional history that had been in fashion in the later nineteenth century. But incarceration in a German prisoner-of-war camp almost certainly gave him the opportunity to reflect on the rhythms of historical time. (There is a telling parallel with Fernand Braudel who attributes a good deal of his influential historical approach to his experience in captivity during the Second World War.) There is little doubting that the experience widened Pirenne's view of the world, and the dynamic forces underlying all history.

Now before considering this famous case-study, it is necessary to reiterate Jacques Le Goff's point that the written record has many limitations. Le Goff shows that the prohibitions of primitive mentalities (as he describes those of the Early Middle Ages) are carried on well after AD 1000 into a world of feudal (i.e. tributary) relations. In fact it is the resistance to change, as it is expressed in the written documentation, that fascinates Le Goff. But what he reveals are 'taboos', as he calls them, worthy of the kula ring (see chapter 2). He charts the revision of these attitudes as an economic and social revolution altered Europe after the ninth century. The very existence of this mentality, though, as was noted above, necessarily forewarns us against investing too much credibility in the written sources before the ninth century. In other words, it provides a rather doubtful basis for constructing a model for the origins of markets. To some extent Pirenne was aware of this. But many anthropologists and historians have failed to grasp the changing mentalities and their implications, in particular, for economic history.

Pirenne's thesis was constructed on a stage as great as that which had engulfed his world in 1914. He challenged the prevailing Renaisance view that the break between the Roman and medieval worlds occurred in the fourth and fifth centuries. Instead he maintained that Roman civilization withstood the barbarian invasions, and its institutions survived until the seventh century. Only then, with the Arab seizure of North Africa and much of the Mediterranean, did the Classical Age perish. In his opinion the Arabs isolated North-western Europe from its formerly Mediterranean roots and paved the way for the Frankish Empire of Charles the Great (d. 814). The Carolingian movement was something fundamentally new and qualitatively different from the preceding age. The Carolingian empire, based upon the barely Romanized Rhineland, was more closely linked with the Church, and was governed by a peripatetic monarchy which found its revenues not in trade but in land and agriculture. The Carolingians, in Pirenne's view, made the scaffolding of the Middle Ages. Thus he believed that the nadir of towns occurred not in the fifth century, but in the seventh to ninth centuries, when they served no economic purpose. Such trade as existed flowed between trading posts, frequented largely by wandering traders of whom the Frisians are the most renowned. The feeble life of these places was snuffed out by the Vikings from western Scandinavia. Only after their brutal assaults did an urban revival take place. These new towns, he argued, were not primarily local markets, but places engaged in long-distance trade. Many were suburbs of old elite (and earlier, classical) settlements, where a transient mercantile community paused on regular journeys across Western Europe. For Pirenne, the key moment in turning these places into towns was in the eleventh century, when the mobile traders settled down as merchants and patricians. Thereafter the great medieval townscapes took shape, many being barely altered until in the nineteenth century they were overtaken by industrialization.

The details of Pirenne's paradigm have been challenged by an army of scholars. Like all great historians, the measure of his importance can be found in the critiques of his work. These critiques, however, have been restricted by the nature of the sources, and by the way those sources have been used. Hence, there is now general accord with Pirenne that the Late Roman world persisted until the seventh century, but much less accord on the institutions of this age and the role of markets. In particular, Pirenne's monocausal explanation for the division between the classical and medieval worlds - the Arabs - has been seriously challenged. Few now accept such a cataclysmic thesis. Yet, strangely, most scholars still accept the Vikings as the agents of change in the ninth century. This seems to be a grave mistake worthy of the history Pirenne challenged (cf. Randsborg, 1982). As for the rebirth of markets, historians have tended to define the details which Pirenne glossed over to present a picture that is not so strikingly different. Many historians have presented the case for more long-distance trade within Carolingian Europe and between it and the East than Pirenne seems to allow. Some historians have emphasized the importance of the old elite centres as the beginnings of medieval towns. Places like Cologne, Milan and Paris have received special attention which illuminates their continuity throughout the Dark Ages. Most historians concur with Pirenne that the Carolingian age was a world of agrarian regional production in which the Church played a special part. Some would argue, however, that elite estates were far more productive than Pirenne allows, and involved in regional-wide exchanges of surpluses. Others minimize agrarian production, but find it difficult to put an exact scale upon it (Montanari, 1979). It is generally agreed that the ninth century, in the wake of Charles the Great, was the crucible of change. But how this affected urban development remains a mystery - at least, in the terms set out by modern historians. The Vikings, as was noted above, are accredited with a special, catalystic part in the process. Yet this seems highly speculative in view of the explicitly partisan monkish sources, affronted by the pagan assault upon Latin Christendom. Nevertheless, it is clear that the later tenth and eleventh centuries were an age of urban expansion, and few would deny that the roots of European markets are traceable to this period. But whether, as Pirenne argued, the first towns were concerned with long-distance trade and only with time became involved in local and regional commerce is a matter of some dispute.

Two major criticisms can be levelled against Pirenne's thesis. First, it takes little account of the complex regional configurations of Western Europe in the period in question. This induced him to make rather sweeping judgements about the process of market formation. Secondly, as Philip Grierson pointed out in a seminal critique of the Pirenne thesis, there is an urgent need to put some sense of scale upon the complex processes in question, particularly in respect of urban and commercial history (1959). The written sources offer very little support in this respect. Almost certainly, for the reasons Jacques Le Goff describes, there were taboos in this age which essentially mean that the written sources (recorded by churchmen) are highly coloured impressions of the time.

In short, it behoves anthropologists to be extremely cautious of using Pirenne's thesis or, indeed, the many critiques of his work as a model for market formation. Yet, it also behoves anthropologists and historians (as was noted in chapter 1) to remember that most of the data at their disposal on this question are from modern contexts where the role of capitalist world systems is beyond doubt. The attraction of the early medieval European transition is that it occurred in a pre-capitalist environment which was already an ecologically and socially complex part of the world. In other words, this European example offers the opportunity to examine the process of market formation in a successful collection of states as opposed to in those underdeveloped (peripheral, to use Wallerstein's definition) conditions which must be deemed unsuccessful.

Archaeology offers the best means of measuring the scale of urbanism and the regional configurations which illuminate market formation. Traditionally, of course, archaeology has been an antiquarian pursuit focussing principally upon art and architectural history. In this capacity its data have been used to embroider the margins of the debate about Pirenne's thesis. But the archaeology which is transacted upon a regional scale, on the recent American model, can draw upon not only the rich European antiquarian tradition but a range of scholars concerned with the many cultural and economic aspects of Europe in the first millennium. The brief examples cited in foregoing pages illustrate exactly this point. A long and very reputable tradition of urban archaeology, supplemented by recent regional fieldwork makes it possible to take an entirely new stance on the Pirenne thesis. Using the models of exchange and market-forms outlined in chapter 2 and in the first half of this chapter, it is possible to chart the evolution of marketing. What these patterns mean, of course, as has been indicated already, are open to debate. But by measuring the processes the anthropology of market formation sheds new light on the political process as the West European nation-states took shape. Therefore the following pages will examine the origins and evolution of the market (rather than its classical demise) first in continental Western Europe and then in two secondary territories – England, Denmark and Ireland.

First, it is clear that classical towns and their hinterlands in France, West Germany and Italy experienced a quite tremendous collapse between the later fifth and early seventh centuries. By AD 700 it appears that only the regional and to some extent central market-places (to use Skinner's typology: see above) of the Roman period had survived. Virtually all intermediate, standard and vegetable-level markets had disappeared. Closer archaeological inspection of these surviving centres shows that they were shadows of their former (classical) places. Tours (France) is a well-studied example (Galinié 1988). This was a 200 hectare Roman regional capital. In the seventh–tenth centuries it comprised a famous but small monastery and a palace from which the surrounding middle Loire was controlled. The material culture associated with these nuclei attests the persistence of limited commodity production, but the scale of these settlements strongly suggests that it was destined primarily for the elite.

Regional studies from areas as diverse as Limburg (Slofstra et al, 1982) and Molise, Italy (Hodges, 1988b) suggest a remarkably undeveloped landscape with minimal agricultural production above subsistence needs and very restricted inter-regional commerce. Both observations lend support to Pirenne's sweeping vista of Dark Age Europe. So too does the evidence of great emporia or *wiks* through which long-distance trade was managed. Some of these have already been described in chapter 2. In essence, these settlements were expressions of controlled long-distance exchange and, simultaneously, places where craft-production might be administered as well. In other words, sites like Dorestad (in the Rhine delta) and Quentovic (the early medieval predecessor of modern Boulogne) encompassing 50 hectares or more were gateway communities where the incoming flow of prestige goods and the outgoing flow of manufactured commodities were managed. But these places were principally ports for the ruling elite and not expressions of regional production-distribution systems. Their exclusive character altered from time to time, in step with the political configurations. But nevertheless these were essentially passage points from which the ruling elite attempted to acquire valuables with which to manipulate their systems.

These places and the evidence from the European regions attest to the first steps in transition from gift-exchange between kin-groups towards commodity production and the evolution of tributary, state arrangements. The concentration of the emporia along the North Sea littoral between the Seine and Hamburg reflects, as Pirenne deduced, the emergence of a core community in the Rhine-Seine axis. The development of this axis can be measured fairly accurately in the archae-ological record, to shed light on Charles the Great's role in the process of market formation (Hodges, 1982).

At the end of the eighth and in the early years of the ninth centuries the regional character of the Rhineland altered. These changes in the core (to use Wallerstein's terminology) were diffused in an irregular pattern to the other West European territories over the next half-century. These seem to have involved the aggrandizement of elite settlements in places like Cologne (Borger, 1985) as a strident political ideology was embodied in buildings and associated facilities.

Market-places as such were not apparently created. In the surrounding countryside some evidence points to the emergence of medieval crop-rotation and field management. Agricultural production, in short, was being intensified in the heartland of the new Holy Roman Empire. Coinage was being promoted as a regular mechanism for exchange (Grierson, 1965), and new aggregated craft-production centres making glassware, pottery, millstones and probably wooden containers are a feature of the age. Cost-control factors were being introduced in order to regulate the investment of labour (energy) and materials more efficiently (see chapter 4 for a further examination of this theme). The artefacts themselves attest the emergence of commodity exchange on a less restrictive scale. Warendorf, a Westphalian village excavated in the 1950's (Winklemann, 1954), was in receipt of a large quantity of Rhenish Carolingian manufactured commodities, as was the contemporary Dutch village of Kootwyk (Heidinga, 1985). Similar evidence of regional development programmes (to use an appropriate EEC phrase) exist in the Beauvaisis and middle Loire areas of France; in the Po plain and in parts of Central Italy; and in much of Flanders. But no evidence presently exists to document any change in the formulation of the regional centres. Cologne, like Tours and Milan, remained a small settlement (by classical standards) surrounded by overgrown monumental Roman ruins. In sum, if markets were held at these places Bohannan and Dalton would classify them as peripheral (see chapter 1).

But places like Dorestad did change. The excavators at Dorestad have documented the increase in long-distance exchange during this period, as its traders handled the new lines of manufactured products. Moreover, the settlement was conspicuously zoned in this phase, with space becoming a critical resource. Dorestad comprised three major parts: the riverside moorings, the warehouses/riverside properties and an agrarian nucleus. The riverside properties were quite different in form to the Frisian farms in the nucleus. These, in fact, are the antecedents of town and country dwellings.

Notably the warehouses/riverside properties betray the existence of individuals marking their bounds and evidently in competition to some extent with the ruling elite.

The dendritic central-place reflects the escalating shift from a kin-based community to a tributary one where commodity control is of central significance to an aspiring sector of the society. From it traders journeyed to less developed territories in the North, where raw materials like slaves, furs, ivory and amber could be found that were held in some esteem by the Carolingian elite. Hence, Dorestad also reflects that at the point of regional transition increased emphasis was given to prestige goods. These circulated amongst the elite as traditional media for establishing and maintaining relations. As will be apparent, these two concurrent routes to economic development were to a large extent contradictory. A classic 'Big Man', Charles the Great, was able to command such aspirations by keeping a tight rein on the lower-ranking elite and by promoting the Church to propagate his (or at least his court's) perspective of the world. But his legacy was fragile, and as is often the case the polity fell apart with internecine warring. The decline of administered long-distance trade accentuated stress within the West Scandinavian communities, which were compelled to seek their resources by raiding those with whom they had previously traded. The spiral of instability was thus set in motion.

Out of the ninth-century crucible grew a variagated pattern of new communities, each undeniably scarred by the Carolingian experience. The Rhineland became the heart of a smaller territorial entity, as did, for example, the Po plain of northern Italy. In these new territories the Carolingian achievement was effectively advanced. Tenth century agrarian and commodity production was developed as Charles appears to have envisaged. Moreover, judging by mint output as well as archaeological evidence, towns like Cologne and Milan evolved as solar central-places administering tentative peasant marketing systems. In other areas that once belonged to the Carolingian Empire the process evolved more slowly. Competition between the lower ranking elites in France, in particular, hindered social and economic development including the rise of market towns. Hence, Carolingian Tours, for example, remained largely unaltered until the formation of a large market town in the later eleventh or early twelfth centuries.

The regional pattern of market formation varied enormously, as critics of Pirenne have indicated. Moreover, those areas that did evolve, such as the Rhineland, took advantage of regional conditions and, to judge from the archaeological, documentary and numismatic sources, had no truck with long-distance trade. Tenth-century Europe, consequently, was the nadir of the middleman. In this respect, Pirenne was well wide of the mark.

The next stage in the formation of medieval market systems remains less clearly defined. It is fairly certain that primate centres were superseded by interlocking central-place markets during the eleventh and twelfth centuries. These ranked market-places, however, may have been in response to what Fernand Braudel has identified as the beginnings of the modern world system (1984: 92). For at the turn of the millennium the Mediterranean Sea, the stagnant Moslem pond (to paraphrase Pirenne), once more came to life. Hitherto, since late Roman times, trade in this region appears to have been on a tiny scale, though by the ninth century it was of critical importance for such gateway communities as Venice, Marseilles, Naples and Sousse. The archaeological evidence for medieval trans-Mediterranean connections only appears clearly from the eleventh century. The material evidence seems to chart the rapid growth of great seabord cities like Pisa and Venice. This growth appears to coincide with the rapid expansion of the regions served by these ports. In Braudel's opinion the great wool fairs of Champagne were the first focal points from which the rest of Western Europe was dominated. This is a contentious assertion which fails to take full account of the very varied regional development of Europe in the tenth and eleventh centuries. But all the sources demonstrate the swift growth of North-west Europe, and its connection with the growing markets of the Mediterranean may have contributed to its development.

Archaeology, therefore, indicates that primate centres were a prominent feature of the pre-state conditions of the Carolingian age. These centres, however, were indisputably linked to the maintenance of traditional economies even though they generated the need for commodity production and new regional development. These dendritic central-places were ephemeral settlements, vulnerable to political change. Dorestad and Quentovic both disappeared with the collapse of the Carolingian system. Instead, the new market-places evolved from the primitive solar central-places which now became regional primate centres (of the $k=7$ variety) before spawning (so-to-speak) ranked competitive markets (of the $k=3$ variety) (see above, pp. 65–66).

The pattern of market formation in the secondary territories beyond the Carolingian frontiers also merits discussion. Above all it provides a glimpse of diffusion rather than imperialistic dominance in a world characterized by complex kin-based relations.

Markets were introduced to England from the Continent. The Roman colony was a distant memory for the patchwork quilt of territories when late in the sixth century the Kentish and perhaps the East Anglian and West Saxon kings forged irregular, small-scale prestige goods exchange relations with Continental traders. The christian missions of AD 597 to Kent, like those to the Pacific in the wake of adventurers such as James Cook, brought an ideology which included limited commodity production and exchange. The primitive, divisive and insular ethos of early post-Roman Britain was challenged (Hodges, 1988a). The scale of trade increased modestly and type A gateway communities were created at places like Ipswich in East Anglia (see chapter 2). These were places on frontiers where trade might be transacted periodically with strangers. But as on the Continent the need for prestige goods gave way to the growing regional demand amongst the elite for more craft products. The type B emporia, of which

Hamwih is the classic example, were constructed to serve this purpose. As we saw in chapter 2, this was a dendritic central-place situated on the edge of a territory which practised gift-exchange. It marks the beginnings of the medieval market: a place to which regional traders might come to obtain a limited range of commodities in highly circumscribed circumstances.

The development of Hamwih tends to reflect the stable political status of the West Saxon leadership. No such stability appears to typify the other kingdoms before the late eighth century. By that time Carolingian ideology was being interpreted by numerous competitive Anglo-Saxon leaders. Simultaneously agrarian and commodity production were overhauled as an attempt to generate controlled regional production from these primate centres. This had been to some extent achieved by the mid ninth century when the crisis caused by the Carolingian collapse and the subsequent Viking raids unfolded. In other words, the preconditions for an economic take-off had been more effectively created than, for example, within the Carolingian realms. But the nexus of change was political. The Viking assault provided the West Saxons with the opportunity to implement a policy that was probably sketched out by Charles the Great. Primate centres like Winchester as well as middle-ranking (central/intermediate) markets like Chichester and Gloucester were planned late in King Alfred's reign in the immediate aftermath of his victory over the Danes, and like latter-day Milton Keynes these planned towns were gradually filled with artisans in the first half of the tenth century. Lower-ranking market-places like Wareham and Wallingford were planned at about the same time, but probably emerged in the mid to later tenth century. Minor market-places (for vegetable exchanges) never developed during Anglo-Saxon times, but may have existed as *loci* for periodic exchange.

The West Saxon pattern was closely followed in the hitherto less developed half of England under Scandinavian control. There is some evidence that the Viking kings of the Danelaw territories (ceded to them by King Alfred) brought in artisans and moneyers in order to stimulate urban development to match the West Saxon achievement. Economic take-off embraced most parts of Late Saxon England by AD 1000, and owed almost nothing to exogenous influence. The result was the development of an underdeveloped countryside coordinated through a system of interlocking competitive markets. Such was the speed and apparent ease with which this transition formed that the Anglo-Saxon kings stand out as powerful monarchs, drawing upon an extraordinarily wealthy landscape.

In sum, the concept of marketing at its most primitive was selectively introduced to English kings about AD 600. Dendritic central-place markets functioned first as gateway communities for administering prestige goods, before becoming monopolistic centres for controlled regional/territorial production. Drawing upon Carolingian technological and economic experience the preconditions for a commercial take-off pre-dated the Viking assault. The successful repulsion of the assault proffered the opportunity to alter the social rules, introducing tributary relations and state apparatus in an explicit pursuit of stabilizing dynastic conditions. Regional primate centres – solar central-places – soon supported by other tiers of markets introduced the market principle to society at large and invoked a great social, economic and technological revolution in all respects (cf. Hodges, 1988a).

Unlike England, Denmark had not been a Roman colony. Prehistory ends with the emergence of its towns in the eleventh century. The origins of these market-places follows the pattern observed in England. Carolingian trading overtures in the eighth century undoubtedly triggered social changes within Denmark. Small type A trading-places at Ribe and Hedeby (the south settlement) attest the growing significance of these connections. With the expansion of Carolingian aspirations, and in particular with the creation of Baltic Sea connections with the Abbasid Caliphate in the Orient, Denmark appreciated that it was at the junction of two trading networks. The famous incident recalled in the Frankish Annals in which King Godfred of the Danes challenged the

Carolingians and concurrently founded Hedeby (or Haithabu, as it is known in Germany: see chapter 2) is almost certainly a garbled account of the bold assertion of Danish rights in this lucrative trade in prestige goods. This at least seems to explain, to paraphrase the Frankish chronicler, why Godfred suddenly raided the trading-place at *Reric* in a neighbouring territory allied to the Carolingians, and kidnapped the merchants he found there. These he then brought to *Sliastorp* (Hedeby), a place situated on the Danish border shared with the Carolingians. The subsequent expansion of Hedeby as a planned emporium of the type B category reflects the growing status of the Danish political system as it forged its axial role for a brief, but highly important phase. The demise of the great cycle of trading networks, therefore, endangered not just the emporium but the political system as a whole.

Finely dated levels (using dendrochronology) within Hedeby indicate that, despite the downturn in long-distance trade between the Baltic Sea and the Orient and between the Carolingians and the Danes, the settlement continued to function. New merchants quarters, for example, were being constructed as Danish armies were in conflict with King Alfred in Wessex. A strong case exists for claiming that the western Scandinavian system turned to raid largely in response to the failure of their trading connections. Whether or not raid satisfactorily replaced trade in obtaining resources is open to question. The political conflict and migrations from Denmark suggest to some extent that an era of political instability followed the breakdown of this mini-world system. But for a generation in the early tenth century the connections between the Baltic Sea and the Caliphate were revived. It is evident that in contrast to the early ninth-century circumstances this time much more of the prestigious goods were retained within the Scandinavian orbit. The Viking cemeteries of Scandinavia, in particular, are awash with exotic items as well as silver. Hedeby as a result seems to have flourished once again, and at this stage the emporium was inhabited by a range of craftsmen making prestige goods. But the oriental connection was again jeopardized in the mid tenth century. Once again a downswing in the volume of commerce occurred. This time King Harald Bluetooth (King of Jutland, if not the whole of Denmark) sought to emulate the Ottonian dynasty of Germany by seeking christian support to alter the fabric of Danish society. One apparent consequence of this was the decline (though not the absolute demise) of Hedeby and the construction of several grand (by Danish standards) palatial complexes or fortresses. Trelleborg and Fyrkat are the most familiar of these perfectly round walled enclosures, each containing four quadrants occupied by impressive long-houses.

Klavs Randsborg has mapped the distribution of these fortresses and the associated material culture of this transitory age. The fortresses appear to be primate centres, each designed as a regional centre. These fortresses coincide with a phase of spectacular burial rights (including the final period of boat-burials) in northern Jutland and with strident property marking in Scania. Randsborg interprets these associated circumstances as indices of the formation of the Danish state, forged during Harald Bluetooth's reign. The fortresses, he argues, are administrative centres – solar central-places –where primitive marketing was being exclusively controlled, while the tribes in northern Jutland and Scania came to terms with their inexorable political fate.

But how did the first market system form? By all accounts it was created after another period of raiding on Anglo-Saxon England. Harald's son and successor, Sven Forkbeard, led a series of campaigns against England and between c.990 and 1015 forced the Anglo-Saxons (and their unfortunate king, Ethelred the Unready) to pay a great ransom, familarly known as Danegeld. Dendrochronology has been used to date the earliest phases of Danish towns like Lund and Roskilde to precisely this period. These were undeniably small places, but to judge from the incidence of coins as well as the voluminous debris of workshops, the market principle was installed and functioning within a short space of time. Notably, copies of Ethelred's pennies were an important feature of the early phases of these market-places. In other words, the Danes saw that a medium of exchange was integral to the efficient development of a market system, as well as for maintaining the apparatus of state power. Cold-bloodedly, instead of drawing upon German experience or the opinions of those by now distant Danish relatives in England, they set about wringing the vital resources from the Anglo-Saxons by force. By the 1020's primate markets functioned in each part of the new Danish kingsdom, several with moneyers actually brought from Anglo-Saxon England. As these new peasant market-places took shape so the tradition of the Vikings slipped into memory, and the nation became concerned with its insular agricultural development (cf. Andrén, 1985).

The origins of the Danish market reveal a sequence not dissimilar to the Anglo-Saxon one to begin with. But Hedeby never developed as a craft-production centre on any great scale. It appears, instead, to have been controlled by trader-farmers who in turn were periodically dominated by the ruling elite, and at other times at odds with the elite. Accordingly, the centre was very sensitive to the ups and downs of the wider trading networks connecting the North Sea to the Baltic. It appears, therefore, that the market system was developed from the conscious construction of new administrative primate centres, which in turn after two generations were consciously made into peasant markets. Kingship and the endogenous development of these new means of managing resources go hand in hand. But as in England, the first markets were extremely small. Little over a hundred persons at most occupied Lund, for example. Demographic factors clearly had little to do with this momentous transition.

The Irish, by contrast, never forged either primate or competitive marketing systems. In common with Denmark, Ireland benefitted from contacts with the Romans but was never drawn within its orbit. Early Frankish connections with Irish chieftains almost prompted emporia like Dalkey Island in the mouth of the River Liffey, but their remains, as such, are very ephemeral. The Norwegians constructed Hedeby –

like longports at Dublin, Wexford, Waterford, Cork and Limerick. Excavations at Dublin attest clearly this tenth-century imitation of the Jutish emporium. By the eleventh century it appears that Dublin had fixed trading connections with western England. But these longports had no impact beyond the limited hinterlands under their control. Moreover, no coinage system evolved either for use within these centres or for their territories. Most of Ireland remained tribal, hierarchical and rural up until the advent of the Anglo-Norman conquest in the late twelfth century. Archaeology, however, demonstrates the advent of the imperialist. At this time a network of castles was swiftly followed by the construction of primate centres (most of them like Downpatrick, Trim and Armagh with previous royal or ecclesiastical association). Coinage was soon produced at these places, and craftsmen in some cases were shipped from England to set up shop – to articulate an underdeveloped economy. The early thirteenth century chronicler, Giraldus Cambriensis leaves us with an anthropologist's impression of a primitive society brought to heel by the civilizing English.

The moral of the Irish condition merits a brief note. Despite cross-Channel trade connections, despite the Norwegian colonies and their famed emporia, and despite relations between the Irish Church and the eleventh- and twelfth-century continental Church, the Irish did not create any form of endogenous market system. Moreover, they failed to attract any exogenous support before the Anglo-Normans arrived. This is an indictment of the political system, fractured between a multitude of so-called kingdoms by an archaic inheritance system, and mightily controlled by the Church. One of the densest populations in any first millennium territory was unable to generate even the most ephemeral levels of marketing.

The formation of market systems in late first millennium Europe is far more complex than Pirenne envisaged. By outlining the process, even in this abbreviated fashion, it will be apparent that territory by territory social forces instigated different economic strategies. Clearly, the articulation of wider economic connections endorsed centralized leadership. But the short-lived, often generation-long character of these arrangements as often as not created political instability as well. In no case did long-distance trade give way to regional marketing. Instead, peasant markets appear to have been formulated as a calculated political strategy, as part and parcel of the dynastic aspirations embodied in the new nation states. It has to be stressed that the Roman past was bound to have been some influence upon these economic strategies – even in tenth-century Europe. (The absence of written evidence of this, bearing in mind the taboos relating to economic affairs, cannot be taken to disprove this connection over the centuries.) Nevertheless, we may conclude that the so-called Polanyi school (to return to Carol Smith's comparison: see above, p. 77) may have identified the factors which triggered political and economic advance from kin-based towards tribute-based societies. But the emergence of market systems occured as an endogenous response to circumstances arising largely as the long-distance connections collapsed. It might be wiser to argue that this model is close to the French neo-Marxist school of anthropologists than to Adam Smith, but this is semantics.

On one matter the European history is clear: as we noted in Ireland, the market was seen as an instrument in the apparatus of state control. This leads us to speculate how the market as such interacted most efficaciously with particular regions in the medieval period to the optimum advantage of the ruling elite. This will be the subject of chapter 5 after the components of early market systems have been considered in more detail.

# 4

# Money and primitive markets

The economic historian, Joseph Schumpeter once claimed that 'There is no denying that views on money are as difficult to describe as shifting clouds' (1954: 289). The interpretation of money in primitive and early state societies is a particularly controversial issue. A good deal of this controversy, as Keith Hart has eloquently shown, is rooted in the confusion about money in our own time (Hart, 1986). Most of us have access to five types of money – coins, notes, cheques, savings accounts and plastic credit cards. The relationship between the five types is inherently unstable. Coins containing precious metals equivalent to their nominal value are uncommon. Base metal coins and paper notes have superseded coinage of this form. Base metal coinage was introduced after the Second World War so that both paper and metal versions of the national currency are strictly worthless, being distinguished by their function rather than the cost of their production. Since the war too, personal cheques and plastic credit cards have been increasingly important means of deploying income in the market-place. In Hart's opinion the coin in one's pocket is most instructive on modern as past monetary theory. On one side is 'heads' – the symbol of the political authority which minted and issued the coin. On the reverse side will be found precise information on the value of the coin as payment in exchange. The obverse declares that the state guarantees the currency; that money represents some form of relation between persons in society. The reverse side reveals the coin to be an object, 'capable of entering into definite relations with other things, as a quantitative ratio independent of the persons engaged in any particular transactions' (1986: 638). Money in this sense is like a commodity, a feature of anonymous competitive markets. The two sides of the coin, according to Hart, stand for social organization from the top down and from the bottom up, epitomized by the state and market. The temptation in modern society, and the temptation when studying past societies, Hart contends, is to adopt a one-dimensional approach to money. Yet, in practice, money is simultaneously an aspect of relations between persons, and an object detached from persons. In short, while taking note of the shifting interpretations of money, and its importance for early markets, we must arrive at a definition that embodies the two sides of the coin.

In this chapter I wish to consider the place of money in primitive markets, taking heed of Hart's thesis. I shall begin by discussing some of the many studies of this problem, a good number of which tend to opt for 'one side of the coin' rather than the other. Following this, I intend to describe the inception of cash in early medieval Europe.

Just about every leading historian, philosopher and anthropologist has spent a few words on money. Nineteenth-century political economists like Ricardo, Mill and Marx believed that money was the servant of the 'law of Value', a technical prerequisite of commodity exchange which should be removed as far as possible from the threat of political interference by being related to precious metals (Hart, 1986: 643). Marx in *Das Capital* (1976), for example, makes it clear that money is a commodity to be used to facilitate exchange, while capital is accumulated money within the exchange system. But Marx also appreciated that money was also a social agent. He demonstrated how money expresses and makes possible the relationships of class-divided as opposed to kin-based societies. Money brought anonymity to exchange. Marx distinguished between the use-value and exchange-value of money, but contended that the philosophy of money does not exist without the commodity market of which it is a part. In sum, Marx's thesis amounts to the view that money relates not only to the emergence and development of stratification in agrarian societies but also to the circulation of commodities within those societies.

In Marx's opinion, all commodity production involves the commensurate exchange of items which are incommensurables. The goods have use-values, but the exchange-values which define them as commodities differ from one another quantitively. Money is the mechanism for expressing this quantification. All commodities, he believed, have a double existence as natural products and as items which have exchange-value. The process of circulation of commodities can only reach a truly integrated economic state if exchange-value becomes detached from products and exists as a separate entity – in the form of money. In this respect, Marx reasoned, the development of monetary systems parallels writing: both are abstractions divorced from those things to which they refer. Writing embodies the movement from pictures to abstract marks that bear an arbitrary relationship to the real world. Similarly, money begins as objects or products that have use-value, become implicated in exchange and thereafter are progressively removed from the original use value of their contents. Marx accordingly deemed money to be a commodity, the true essence of which is intrinsically worthless, but embodies the exchange-value of all other commodities (Giddens, 1981: 116).

The origins of money and its place in primitive and peasant economics was not, of course, Marx's primary concern. Nevertheless, his views have had a great influence on twentieth-century anthropologists. In particular, some have sought to separate the exchange and use-values – the heads and the tails, as Hart puts it, in primitive currencies. For instance, Mary Douglas and Marshall Sahlins in their rather different approaches to primitive (pre-market) exchange have located the origins of currency systems in exchange. Douglas distinguished two types of primitive currencies: firstly, general purpose currencies in which the currency unit is employed as a mechanism of exchange without restriction; and secondly, primitive rationing systems where the unit is deployed to control the distribution of prestige goods, in order to reinforce the social order (1967). Sahlins believes that 'primitive money' amounts to those objects which have token rather than use value in pre-state societies and, consequently, serve as mechanisms in exchange (Sahlins, 1974: 227). More specifically, Sahlins means that exchange use is restricted to the acquisition of certain categories of objects, though land and labour are ordinarily excluded. This type of exchange, he believes, only takes place between parties of certain social relation.

Hart offers a more complex explanation for exchange tokens in such political and economic circumstances. Taking Malinowksi's famous study of the kula ring in *Argonauts of the Western Pacific* (1922), he shows how the two sides of this exchange circuit in fact reinforced each other (Hart, 1986: 647-9). Malinowksi's book describes the cycle of trading between the far-flung islands of the Trobriand archipelago. A central aspect of his study is the contrast between *kula* and *gimwali* in the Trobriand economy. *Kula* is a ceremonial exchange of personal ornaments between the leaders (big men) of the visiting islanders and their hosts, carrying great social prestige; *gimwali* is an undignified haggling which occurred between the lower orders of the two communities at the same time as, but out-of-sight of, the *kula* ceremony. The one epitomized generosity, the other a personal selfishness. Hart argues that the ceremony, designed to overcome a good deal of danger and magic, yet imbued with the ethos of prestige and hierarchy, amounts to a temporary social framework erected in the relative absence of a notion of society. By contrast, the haggling on the beaches between islanders eager to exchange their commodities for those from another environment in the Trobriands is an illustration of how individuals from both groups feel free to risk conflict. In Hart's opinion, *gimwali* is a small-scale interaction predicated on the temporary presence of society, and thus the individualism of the bartering is

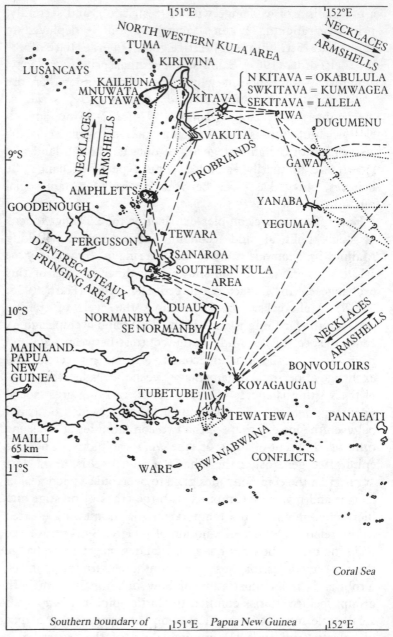

**Figure 9** *A map of the kula ring in the 1970's compiled by G. Irwin and J. Leach. Source: Leach, 1983.*

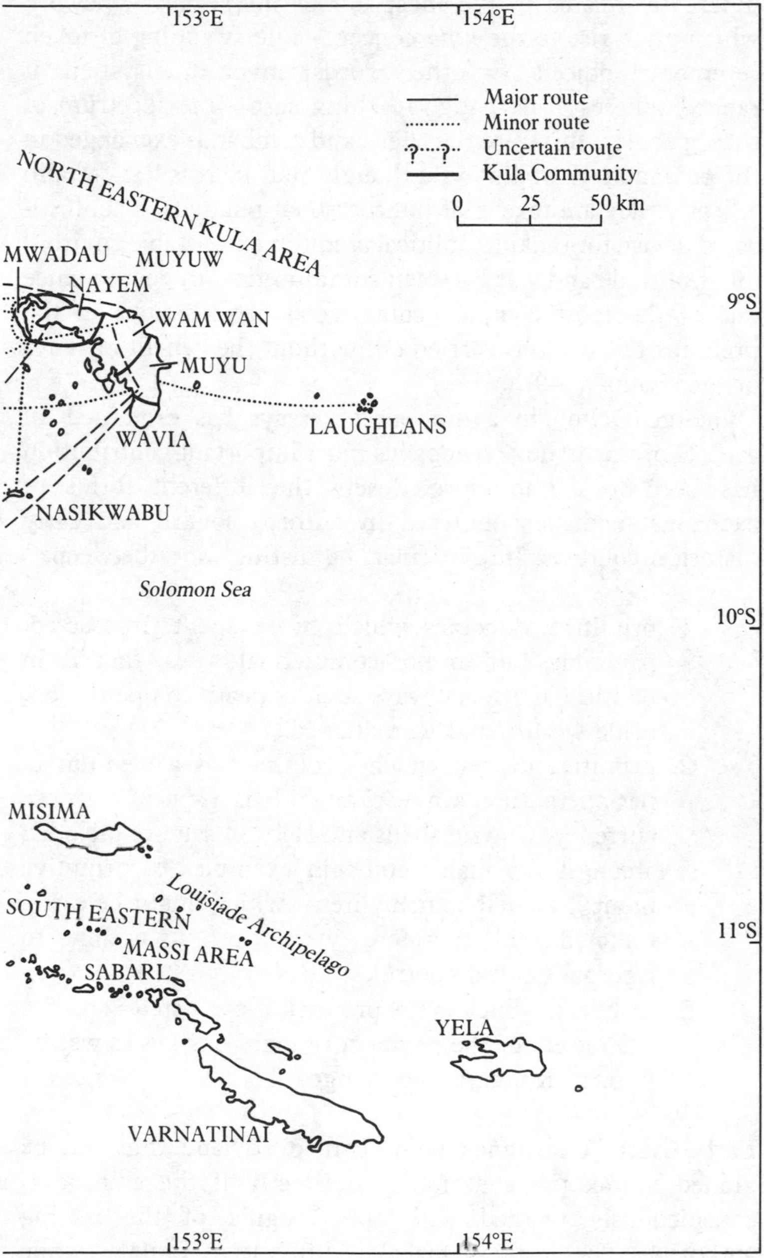

153°E
154°E
Major route
Minor route
Uncertain route
Kula Community
0
25
50 km
NORTH EASTERN KULA AREA
MWADAU
MUYUW
NAYEM
WAM WAN
MUYU
WAVIA
LAUGHLANS
NASIKWABU
Solomon Sea
9°S
10°S
11°S
MISIMA
Louisiade Archipelago
SOUTH EASTERN
MASSI AREA
SABARL
YELA
VARNATINAI
153°E
154°E

inherently related to the inception of the social framework which gives rise to the *kula* concept. The swapping of token ceremonial objects, in other words, invoked a system of ranked spheres of exchange reaching across the spectrum of these peoples. But were the shells and armbands exchanged in the *kula* money? Malinowski thought not. Hart is less certain. 'Clearly they are tokens of interpersonal relations, a sophisticated device for ranking political credit in an unstable environment of trade and war between communities. In consequence one of the most complex commercial organisations in the preindustrial world is carried out without the benefit of states or merchants' (649).

George Dalton in a number of essays has examined all aspects of this issue. Perhaps his most important contribution has been to define more closely the different forms of exchange media encountered in anthropological and early historical contexts. In particular, he distinguishes between:

1. primitive valuables which 'were spent, transacted, paid out, but in non-commercial ways, that is in political and social ways such as death compensation, bride wealth, and war alliance';
2. primitive money which is defined as a medium in peripheral (non-kin) exchange. It is a special-purpose currency. Cowrie shells and slabs of salt are included amongst the many non-coin examples of primitive money, as well as many items which might be easily imitated and therefore were not susceptible to rigorous central control, and;
3. early cash which is the product of early states and has been used for the payment of taxes or fines as well as in ordinary market exchange.

Early use of cash tends to be controlled, and thus can be graded to tax the community indirectly if the coinage is conspicuously marked with the insignia of the issuing authority. The insignia make it difficult to imitate, while rulers invariably legislate against forging. Dalton's framework is useful in historical discussions as it offers a direct and simple association between monetary and political development.

One stage on from the early use of cash is all-purpose money, the cash of the fully-developed commodity market system in which Marx was principally interested. It is useful to see how anthropologists, obviously influenced by Karl Marx as well as modern economists, treat this category of medium of exchange. Marvin Harris in his textbook on anthropology describes all-purpose money as possessing the qualities of:

1. Portability. It comes in sizes and shapes convenient for being taken from one transaction to the next.
2. Divisibility. Its many forms and values are multiples of each other.
3. Convertibility. A transaction made in a higher-value unit can be made equally well in lower-value multiples.
4. Generality. Virtually all goods and services have a monetary value.
5. Anonymity. For virtually all purchases, any person with the appropriate money can make a transaction.
6. Legality. The nature and quantity of money in circulation will be controlled by the state (Harris, 1980: 239–40).

All-purpose money of the many-faceted kind described here is extremely rare in peasant societies, and absent from pre-state societies. These like a fully-integrated commodity market are features of western capitalist systems. Early cash, by contrast, possesses some of these attributes, but it never becomes entirely synonomous with commodities in the sense that Marx had in mind. Indeed, even in comparatively recent times European peasant systems have treated money as a bullion, stored to purchase those commodities which cannot be made in the domestic context (see below: p. 121). In short, the history of money like the concept of value is far from straightforward. Like the history of market-exchange, it is an oversimplification to impose a rigid behavioural straightjacket on a most complex phenomenon.

## From primitive valuables to early cash

As we have seen, there is a strong feeling that primitive valuables and, thereafter, currencies evolve from contacts with distant or non-kin relations either within a territory or between territories. Hence, it is believed that the shell-using societies of Melanesia, for example, were adapting to wider, more extensive economic systems. These items were media in complex exchange systems. As I have pointed out in chapter 1, the ethnocentric view of isolated and 'simple' aboriginal societies is neither borne out by prehistory nor by anthropology. Balanced reciprocity was an important feature of band and tribe levels of society, fulfilling social needs (Bender, 1978). Control over valuables, accordingly, is an expression of the embryonic political economy: hence there are systems in which 'big men' disperse the valuables, and others where centralized leadership includes the accumulation of valuables (cf. the discussion of withdrawal and dispersal systems in chapter 2). The obvious difficulty in regulating values like shells, tusks or ingots seems not to have detracted from their place in society. A common unit of value in primitive societies is a cow, for example. Many Iron Age African societies equated cattle and wives. But cattle are not divisible. As employed in *bride-price* cattle cannot be converted into other creatures. Usually cattle lack generality since only wives can be purchased with them, and they lack anonymity because not just any person can arrive, produce the cattle, and carry off a wife. Instead, cattle are indices employed between kin or pre-arranged alliances where the intention is to forge or reinforce relations. Finally, cattle are put into circulation by each individual household as a result of its productive efforts; consequently, no means (in theory) exists to regulate this resource.

The limitations of primitive valuables like cattle must be compared with the complex features of primitive money. For example, the Rossel Islanders in Melanesia use a shell money which has on occasions been confused with early cash currencies. The shells are obviously portable, and they occur in 22 named units of value (nos 1-22). These units fall into three classes: numbers 1 to 10, numbers 11 to 17, and numbers 18 to 22. A person who borrows a number 1 shell must return a number 2. Number 2 must be repaid with a number 3, and so on. This continues through to shell number 9. But a person who borrows a number 10 cannot be obliged to return a number 11. Thus the series 1 to 10 is divisible; this series is also fairly generalized as it can be used to acquire items such as buckets and pots. But the two series 1 to 10 and 11 to 17 are neither divisible nor convertible with regard to one another. In the same way the series 18 to 22 is different as well. There are only some 60 shells in this series in circulation, and they are incovertible with respect to the other (lower order) series. Hence, shell number 18 is the only shell that can be used for wife purchase or for sponsorship of a pig feast. Number 20 similarly, is the only shell that can be used as an indemnity for ritual murder. George Dalton, with good reason, observes 'It is about as useful to describe a pig feast on Rossel as buying a pig with a no 18 *ndap* as it is to describe marriage in America as buying a wife with a wedding ring' (Dalton, 1965).

One consequence of these distinctions is that it follows from them that 'money' is not constant in its uses or appearance. Conversely, two forms of it may look alike without it following that they were used in the same ways, or in the same forms of society. This helps to explain why the most heated debates on the question of primitive currencies have occurred where money takes a coin-like form. Early hellenic and early medieval European currency have been the subjects of disputes between those who assume that they can be equated with the regulated coinage with which we are familiar, and those familiar with anthropological systems of value who have perceived the sequence from primitive money to early cash to fully fledged currency. As is so often the case, ethnocentric attitudes and a lack of interest in complex socio-economic arguments has limited the impact of what might be termed the anthropological argument.

Recently John F. Cherry and I made an attempt to tackle this problem from a new angle. Since money is explicitly an archaeological phenomenon, we proposed that W. L. Rathje's cost-control model might illuminate the critical transition in Anglo-Saxon coinage. The argument is a lengthy one, but since we were not aware of any detailed and comprehensive statement of the changes to be expected in a coinage system concomitant with increased social and political complexity, it seems pertinent to recount the general assumptions and principles of this model here.

Rathje's model draws on General Systems Theory for its fundamental assumption that 'one of the most obvious properties of an open system in a temporal matrix is that the dynamics of the system's internal matter-energy-information structures change' (Rathje, 1975: 410). In other words, from the materialist perspective of the archaeologist, systems which are growing in size and complexity will generate predictable changes in the form and distribution of the components of their material culture components through time. These changes are predictable because every expanding system growing at a linear rate must introduce some form of compensation for the exponentially expanding need for information processing and deciding components. Rathje argues (1975: 412–16) that one aspect of such compensation is the introduction of techniques to diminish the cost of producing and distributing a commodity (measured in material and energy investment), and so increase the amount produced, and enable it to be distributed more widely. The stress here is on the trend towards mass production and distribution of commodities based on the principles of standardization, simplification, efficiency, reduction of energy/material input, and so on. These are principles familiar, of course, to the conservative western democracies in the 1980s. The introduction of mass replication and distribution techniques transforms the focus of social integration based on systems of production and distribution systems from elite reinforcement by means of high-investment products loaded with psychological and ideological values toward a more direct form of economic integration in which local small-scale production units are superseded by an overarching production and distribution system (Rathje, 1975: 414–15).

There is, therefore, an expectable sequence in the history of an item of material culture in a cultural system of growing complexity: 1) an initial phase of heavy investment in craft production of small numbers of commodities whose spatial and/or social distribution is highly constrained, 2) a phase of mass replication and distribution of standardized commodities that are widely dispersed, and eventually 3) a modification of established cost-control techniques to permit increased local variety in form and distribution.

In a later paper, Rathje (1978) has outlined some ways in which such an approach might be applied to the study of production-distribution systems in the past. Noting the long-term empirically observed tendency of exchange systems in a particular area to switch from long-distance trade to intensive regional exchange and from variable to standardized trade goods, he suggests that diachronic patterns of this kind may be part of an efficient cost-control strategy in which transport costs are minimized by taking ever larger local market shares. As part of the overall growth in the volume of trade, specialized production grows in areas of mass consumption, with concomitant changes in the functions of manufactured items. Reduced to essentials, the expected trend is from '(1) resource concentration into a few labor-intensive forms found dispersed over a wide area to (2) greater quantities of cheaper items more evenly distributed within smaller regions' (1978: 167).

Rathje's perspective of long-running patterns of trade is open to the charge of being reductionist – simplifying historical developments that, as we saw in chapter 3, are much more complex. Nevertheless, his ideas have several implications for the time-trends to be expected in archaeological patterns of coin production, distribution, and function as sociopolitical complexity increases. Let me briefly set out some of these cost-control expectations, before illustrating how these shed light on the exceptionally well-documented case of Anglo-Saxon England and the formation of those markets described in chapters 2 and 3.

1. *The total volume of coinage within the system will increase with political complexity.* It is an obvious corollary of Rathje's cost-control model that the trend towards mass-production will lead to an increase in the output of commodities. Coinage functioning as primitive valuables can be expected to exist only in minute quantities; the shift to early cash, within an expanding market economy, inevitably creates ever-larger demand for coined money with which to perform exchange transactions.

2. *The size of individual coin issues will increase with political complexity.* Rathje's model predicts that, over time, production-distribution networks become more efficient. Since the main overheads to an authority issuing coinage are in the areas of 1) acquiring raw materials, 2) costs of manufacturing dies and striking coins, 3) costs of distribution, and 4) security and control measures to maintain the exchange value of an issue and combat counterfeiting, these are the main areas where streamlining to take advantage of economies of scale may be expected. An obvious cost-control possibility in this respect is to mass-produce large numbers of a single coin type in a single operation, using the same pair of dies until they are too worn for further use; over time, then, the size of an issue, expressed either as the average coin output per die or as the extent to which a die-design is retained without modification beyond the use-life of any actual die, will go up. Where coinage is neither circulating in bulk nor issued by a single central

authority, minting activity will be expedient and sporadic and few dies will be used to capacity. Variability within such smaller issues may well also be expected to be greater than in later, larger issues; the percentage of 'irregular' issues may be larger.

3. *Unit variation within the coinage system will increase with political complexity.* If increased streamlining and mass-production occur (see expectation 2 above), then the fixed overheads of setting up a mint, manufacturing dies and paying moneyers can be spread over a larger overall output of coins, i.e., the cost of making a single coin, regardless of face value, will decrease. This makes possible the widespread introduction of base metal coinages, whose manufacturing cost in relation to actual metallic value is liable to be high. This leads to two expectations: 1) over time, a coinage system based on a single high-value metal (gold/electrum/silver) will be transformed into a system using a number of distinct metals simultaneously and 2) over time, a coinage system using only a single unit of account will transform into a multiple unit system, with relatively fixed standards of conversion from one unit to another (e.g. pounds, shillings, pence). Issuing authorities will be increasingly concerned to ensure that the face value and actual exchange value of these various units remain the same, by maintaining purity standards and manipulating the money supply in response to demand. It is also the case, of course, that until the invention of token coinage in base metals the value of even the smallest denomination is too high for use in exchange transactions in the market-place for everyday essentials. Consequently, it is widely recognized (Collis, 1971) that the appearance of low-denomination, base metal coinage in quantity in the archaeological record is a valid basis for postulating the growth of market-place exchange and the permeation of the economy as a whole by coined money. Early complex societies seem in general to wish to encourage organized (and thus controllable) markets and the widespread use of coins and may do so by deliberately introducing a flexible and widely applicable monetary system. But it is the

economies of scale resulting from mass-production that allows them to do so, and it is for this reason that base metal coinage appears only in developed states. On the other hand, the precious metal content of high-value coins meanst that they do not necessarily require any complex institutional backing.

4. *The organization of coin production will change with increasing political complexity.* Mass-production processes, increased demand for coinage, and the need to service all localities within the state with readily identifiable coins will necessitate the creation of additional mints, the expansion of existing mints, or both. We may legitimately expect to see such changes reflected indirectly in the archaeological record. The actual recognition and archaeological excavation of mints is too rare an occurrence for this pattern to be monitored directly. Ultimately, however, there may be a trend toward one or a few centralized large-scale mints as in Britain today. The numbers of moneyers will also tend to increase and might be reflected in an increasing number of such individuals naming themselves on their respective coin issues. Cost-control factors will encourage the regular spacing of mints throughout the area that these are intended to service, in order to reduce transportation costs. (This might be seen as a corollary to Walter Christaller's marketing principle in central-place theory when $k = 3$ (see chapter 3).) The proliferation of local mints envisaged here as a product of purely economic factors is, however, likely to be distorted by political considerations: both weak and strong central authorities may have good reasons for wishing to exercise closer control of the monetary system by reversing this devolutionary process. With the emergence of the unified nation state and the incorporation of previously autonomous areas, in fact, there may be a trend toward more direct royal control of coin production, for example, by regulating the output rates of each mint or by manufacturing dies at a single central location, from which they are distributed to local mints to use in striking coins.

5. *Individual coin issues will become more standardized with increasing political complexity.* Rathje has suggested that mass replication and the distribution of standardized sets of products characterizes the later phases of the material culture trajectory he has described (1975: 414). The clearest manifestation of this process is likely to be a reduction in the standard deviations of the weight and metallic purity of coins within an issue. If every coin is not to be tested at each exchange transaction to ensure that purity is standard and that the coin has not been clipped or shaved, then steps must be taken to guarantee that all officially stamped coins are indeed exactly equivalent. The actual technology of striking coins may therefore be expected to show some trends toward measures that in some way guarantee both the purity of a coin and protect against fraud either during the minting or subsequent circulation.

6. *The use of coins as a vehicle for propaganda will increase with political complexity.* In a stateless sociopolitical system, the 'message' stamped on coins introduced from more complex foreign polities or on local imitations of such coins is likely to be either irrelevant or incomprehensible to the users of these coins. Notable examples of this are the Celtic imitations of Macedonian philippi, south Arabian imitations of Athenian owl-coinage, and Danish imitations of late Roman gold coins. The circulation of coins in such cases is strictly local and/or socially constrained, the only prerequisite being that their designs should be identifiably distinct from those of other mints or of earlier issues. In nation-states, on the other hand, a coin's guarantee of value is its issuing authority, which bears the costs of coining, of distribution and of quality control. It is for this reason that it is not uncommon for a coin to be worth more than its equivalent weight in bullion within its area of origin and for coins to tend to drain back to the region in which they were issued (Kraay, 1964: 90-1). The growth of a state, of course, involves the progressive incorporation of previously autonomous ethnic or political units and results in exponential growth of information

exchanges and decision-making, as Rathje (1975) amongst many others has noted. These factors suggest that there are likely to be directional changes in the overall design of coins. With mass production, standardization, and far wider circulation patterns, coinage types will become more detailed and specific in order to permit their ready identification in areas remote from the point of issue and where the purely local symbolism of earlier coin types may not be understood. Moreover, since control of the peripheral areas of states inevitably depends as much on persuasion, threat, and ideology as on the direct application of force (Cherry, 1978; Renfrew & Cherry, 1986), coins are bound to take on increased importance as a means of disseminating propaganda and asserting authority widely throughout the population. Testable expectations in this respect include:

1. increasingly common depictions of the face of the king or other charismatic leaders,
2. a trend towards complexity of designs and inscriptions, in excess of the minimum required for simple identification,
3. increased use on coins of privy marks and other accessory symbols solely for the benefit of the administration in checking the authenticity of standardized coinage circulating at some distance from the center of the realm, and,
4. enlargement of the face of the coin (but not necessarily an increase in weight) in order to accommodate all these elements (Hodges and Cherry, 1983: 147-51).

Let me now illustrate how the cost-control model helps to clarify the formation of markets and the history of coin-using in Anglo-Saxon England. The summary that follows owes a good deal to a great number of studies by the numismatists Christopher Blunt, Mark Blackburn, Philip Grierson, Michael Metcalf and Stuart Rigold. A concise and valuable introduction to their work can be found in Grierson and Blackburn, *Medieval European Coinage*, volume 1 (1986).

The minting of coins stopped more-or-less with the departure of the Roman armies from Britain. Post-Roman Britain, therefore, was a moneyless society. Old Roman coins, however, may have circulated within certain spheres of the primitive tribal groupings that made up fifth- and sixth-century Britain. Coins as such were not reintroduced until the later sixth century when the Kentish court obtained them from the Merovingian court(s) on the other side of the English Channel. But before these Merovingian gold coins there came Danish imitation coins - bracteates - which similarly concentrate in Kent. The bracteates embodied the idea of coinage in pendants which appear to have served as a medium in the emerging North Sea tribal relations of the sixth century. By any definition the bracteates were primitive valuables as opposed to any currency, and undeniably important elements in the welding of trade partnerships during this migrationary phase. In the case of England, therefore, these primitive valuables paved the way for the primitive Merovingian currencies.

The Merovingian gold coins were part of the package of prestige goods imported into south-east England through type A gateway communities like Ipswich and one situated beside the Wansum Channel of Kent. This flow of gold also accompanied the Christian missions who sowed the unmistakeable seeds of social change, inducing ultimately not only a new ritual but also (and more significantly) a return in some small measure towards commodity production. This transformation occurred over several generations during the seventh century, culminating as we noted in chapters 2 and 3, with the setting-up of type B emporia (gateway communities) where exchange of regional products as well as prestige goods were enacted. An integral feature of this formative period is that coinage passed through an interesting sequence. First, with the decline in the exchange of prestige goods, the quantity of Merovingian coins coming to Kent fell in the 630s. To buffer themselves against the social perturbations engendered by this, the Kentish court (and possibly the East Saxon and West Saxon courts too) minted their own variants of the hitherto imported primitive currencies. In short, the bullion was needed for social production in these tribes. But in any case the social order was being reshaped. Interestingly, Philip Grierson has argued that some of these indigenous gold types were now being used as indices of blood-prices. Notably, the famous Crondall hoard of c. 650 appears to be precisely the value of a West Saxon ceorl. Hence, change in attitudes to resources also included change in attitudes to human resources. These were measured just as landed and moveable wealth were measured. The late seventh-century laws of King Ina of Wessex, probably the architect of the type B emporium at Hamwih (Saxon Southampton), incorporate these monetary measures quite clearly.

Indeed, the inception of the type B emporium at Southampton, like the escalation in the exchange of prestige goods between other Anglo-Saxon kingdoms and the Continent coincides with the introduction of a much more flexible currency device – the silver *sceatta*. Anglo-Saxon *sceattas* explicitly imitated the Merovingian silver deniers introduced in the later seventh century. There can be little doubt that these were initially dual-function currencies. They circulated within the spheres of international commerce – the prestige goods' exchange networks embracing the North Sea and English Channel zones, and they served as measures within tribal society. But few of these small silver pellet-like coins were marked clearly with the insignia of the minting authority (cf. expectation nos. 5 and 6 above). Instead, curious signs and symbols lend marvellously fine decoration to these objects. Like the shell money they could be imitated, but were they?

The answer is yes. With time the system of *sceatta* production evolved, being imitated not only by many of the numerous Anglo-Saxon tribes, but in all likelihood by competing elites within certain of those territories. The result, to the dismay of numismatists, is an anarchic pattern of coins which occur (in terms of their small size) in striking quantities (cf. expectation no. 1). An inflation in value appears to have ensued as the ranked spheres of exchange were broken down, and as the configurations of trade partnerships entered an unsettled phase. Hence, the second generation of these coins occur principally in inland contexts or within the gateway communities. It appears that the *sceattas* were still employed in trade – but in a much wider network of balanced reciprocity embracing most levels of society. Only in Wessex were the coins restricted: they circulated in astonishing numbers (to judge from their prolific loss) within Hamwih, but seldom outside it (cf. expectation no. 2).

The *sceattas*, therefore, offer a modest intimation of the long-term problems encountered in maintaining a ranked exchange system. Societies are seldom static and the primitive rationing system, as Douglas described it, invariably comes under scrutiny. When it is challenged inflation ensues and the system alters. In this Middle Saxon case, it appears that the strongly centralized economic strategies virtually broke down after a generation of secondary (inflationary) *sceattas*.

Once again a change in the Continental system led to changes in England. For a generation (between c. 760–c. 795) the Anglo-Saxon emulation of the Continental Carolingian ideas was confused. But towards the turn of the century, as several Anglo-Saxon kingdoms built type B gateway communities, a new type of coinage – the penny, efficiently stamped out on a flan – replaced the pellet-type *sceattas*. These coins depict the issuing authority and reflect the switch towards using coinage for regional purposes (cf. expectations nos. 1, 4 and 5).

The inception of competitive market-places after AD 900 went hand in hand with the production of coinage. Moneyers were licensed to operate in most markets – regional and inter-mediate markets often had several active moneyers (cf. expec-tations 1, 2, 4 and 5). The Anglo-Saxon laws demonstrate the close interest taken by the kings in the production of coinage. For a time, towards the end of the tenth century, pennies were issued for six-year periods before being recalled, enabling the

(a)                                               (b)

**Figure 10**    *A BMC type 39 sceatta from Hamwih, Middle Saxon Southampton. This type with the distinctive face on the obverse and spindley bird on the reverse was minted in Hamwih in the period c. 720-50.*
*Illustration reproduced courtesy of Southampton City Museums.*

royal government to control closely the amount of silver in circulation. By AD 1000 Anglo-Saxon England, to judge from its many mints and moneyers, was awash with silver. This fact, it is often said, attracted the second wave of Viking attacks.

In sum, it appears as though primitive valuables like the bracteates were the forerunners of the first primitive currencies: the Merovingian gold tremisses. Both were clearly part of prestige goods' exchange relations between south-eastern kingdoms and those on the Continent. The concepts were seldom adopted by the many other tribes, presumably because they had access to much less gold (being further along the network of trade partnerships) and consequently deployed the gold in ways more suitable to their particular ethnic situations. The currencies were first used to measure blood prices in the wake of the christianization of the English. People like commodities were being valued. But the currencies were highly restricted, even after the switch from a gold to a silver standard. The circulation of coins, however, increased when competing groups sought access to these hitherto closed spheres of economic interaction. Money, accordingly, was commonly found but its value almost certainly was inflated.

The early use of cash can be traced to the type B emporia as these assumed ascribed regional roles. Clearly, the early concept of cash formed an important part of what I have termed the first English Industrial Revolution, during the period from Alfred's reign until the end of the tenth century. The presence of coinage was undeniably an attractive feature of Late Anglo-Saxon England as far as the Danes and Normans were concerned. The strongly-controlled treasury with the effective circulation of currency throughout the kingdom was unique in Western Europe at the turn of the millennium.

The great body of archaeological, historical and numismatic literature for Anglo-Saxon England affords us an unusually detailed view of the transition from primitive valuables to cash. But, does the cost-control model illuminate the process in a way that may be valuable where these interdisciplinary sources are less ample? First, the cost-control model does draw attention to the massive increase in the volume of Anglo-Saxon coinage between c. 600 and 1066. But we were unable to make any precise comparison between the volume of coinage in Middle Saxon times (in the eighth and early ninth centuries) and the Late Saxon period (tenth and eleventh centuries). The spatial evidence for the changes in use reinforces the viewpoint that coinage is not only a medium of distribution, but an explicit expression of production as well. Accordingly, volume of coinage, like the various configurations of market-places, needs to be analyzed in regional terms and alongside other indications of production-distribution systems. Hence, the second expectation – the size of the coin issue – was beyond scientific analysis. The third expectation, concerned with unit variations, is not borne out by the evidence. Very few half-pennies, third-pennies and farthings were minted by Anglo-Saxon moneyers, suggesting that there was little need for fractions of the standard unit. The fourth expectation produced some useful clarity: a case can be made for an early, centrally-controlled Anglo-Saxon coinage (the primary *sceattas*), followed by an uncontrolled, moderately decentralized system (secondary *sceattas*), which was centralized for regional purposes about AD 800 (the first pennies), before being decentralized in a highly controlled system (the tenth-century pennies) to serve the development of competitive markets. The fifth expectation considered the question of standardization. The results show some rigorous control of early (seventh-century) high-value coins. By contrast, the subsequent silver coins display a great deal of variability. This variability terminated with the pennies made from flans after c. 800. The more efficient production of coins on a flan as opposed to on individual pellets evidently made it also easier to achieve a high degree of standardization. It seems that, eventually, the degree of control enabled certain kings to use the fineness of the silver itself as a means of taxation, a measure that fairly illustrates the embeddedness of coinage in Late Saxon society. Sixthly, Anglo-Saxon coins accurately reflect Rathje's point that 'as the growing system faces new communication demands, it will place increasing emphasis upon rigid patterning of sets of interactions' (Rathje, 1975: 414). Hence, the investment in the eighth-century *sceatta* series is inordinately high; King Offa, at a critical transitory stage in the political economy, streamlined the production system, but simultaneously galvanized the artistic skill of the Middle Saxon moneyers to produce eloquent pieces of craftsmanship. By contrast, the moneyers serving the competitive markets of the Late Saxon kingdom are manifestly less skilful, their coins being mechanized objects specifically functional in their purpose. In sum, the cost-control model qualitatively emphasizes the transitory character of the Anglo-Saxon coinage, and as an expression of the political economy serves to confirm the need to examine numismatic data in its holistic rather than its particular context.

It is pertinent to compare the history of currency from another part of early medieval Europe to illustrate the rather obvious point that there were several routes towards the inception of early cash. Birgitta Hardh has investigated the transition from primitive currency to early cash in Scania, southern Sweden – in Viking times an important territory within the Danish polity (Hardh, 1977-78). Hardh's examination of the hoards of valuables to form a picture of the earliest currencies has led her to propose the following sequence:

1. From the later ninth century until about 970 AD the pattern of valuables from the region suggests a heterogenous structure. In the early part of this phase there are hoards whose components all, or almost all originate from the same area. The objects contained in these hoards have been invariably cut up to a very limited degree only. One distinctive group of hoards contains Scandinavian jewellery unevenly cut into large and small pieces. Hardh claims that the variability in the cutting-up of the valuables indicates that the function of the silver was not yet homogeneous.

2. From AD 971- c. 1040 hoards notable for their homogeneity occur. The silver coins in these hoards for example, have been cut into regular fractions of between 1-2 grammes. The same is true of the hacksilver jewellery. In addition, many of the objects have been pecked to test the quality of their silver content. Hardh asserts that these hoards, coinciding in the 1020s onwards with the introduction of standardized silver penny series from the incipient market-places like Lund (in central southern Scania), show a homogeneous nature indicative of intensive regional and even inter-regional circulation. She notes, incidentally, the presence of jewellery from many different Scandinavian regions in these hoards.

3. After AD 1040 the nature of the hoards in south Sweden alters unmistakeably. Hacksilver and foreign coin (much of it collected as Danegeld) are replaced by domestic Danish coins. This transition appears to have been more-or-less completed by c. 1070 - in other words, 50 years or so after the setting up of mints in new towns like Lund.

The Scanian hoards provide an illuminating sequence wherein the transition from primitive valuables to primitive currencies and thence to early cash is far from controlled. Hardh's first phase almost certainly relates to a period in which periodic local markets - peripheral markets in the Dalton and Bohannan typology - were the principle points of exchange. The overt isolation of the region from any wider networks is reflected not only in the heterogenous pattern of hacksilver, but in the absence of imported valuables. The system may have been stimulated by ninth-century inter-regional trade (see chapter 3), but it functioned thereafter independently. This altered in the wake of Harald Bluetooth's political activities in neighbouring Jutland. In period 2, Scania was brought securely within the embryonic Danish state. Still valuables were hoarded, but whilst pennies were minted at Lund, hacksilver too was cut to standardized sizes and weights. Hence, in phase 3 as the market-places slowly took shape, regional exchange was mediated through the use of the newly standardized coins with hacksilver becoming an increasingly rarer feature. Aged Vikings must have witnessed an economic revolution similar to that which finds New Guinean 'big men' compelled to change their investments from pigs to intrinsically worthless paper money (cf. Gregory, 1982). Unlike modern New Guinea, however, the transition occurred over many generations during which each would have been aware of the inexorable shift in the form of trade currencies. The plight of peasant communities in the modern world is to be catapulted across this long unfolding sequence.

But to what extent was early cash used in medieval society? This question perplexes historians and anthropologists alike. Clearly, this form of cash was not freely available in the sense pinpointed by Marx as a vital auxiliary to commodity circulation. Early cash was not an all-purpose currency. So was its use restricted for the purchase of commodities, rather as currencies have been deployed by modern peasantries? Shanin points out, for example, that an absence of cash is a feature of modern peasant systems (1971: 240) In W. I. Thomas and F. Znaniecki's account of Polish peasants, they claim that money was not an exchange medium but just another form of property: 'Money is a relatively new kind of property . . . For the peasant, money property has originally not the character of capital . . . He does not at first even think of making money produce; he simply keeps it at home' (1958: 184). These authors illustrate how money is kept in different spheres: for example that acquired through a dowry must be used to purchase land and nothing else (1958: 165). Paul

Stirling in his description of two Turkish villages confirms this picture; 'Bride price was paid in gold and silver currency, and wealth was stored in gold coins worn as ornaments by the women. On the whole, most villagers marketed little direct, and most of what they did market was bartered with visiting traders for various necessities . . .' (Stirling, 1965: 73). Juliet Du Boulay encountered similar attitudes to cash in a Greek mountain village in Euboea as late as 1966. The villagers distrusted cash, she explains, because of its historical political and economic instability. Former generations kept their money in chests – 'given in dowries, it was to be used as an adornment, it was to be *worn*. It was an indication of the "strength" of the house, and as such it was to be stored, not to say hoarded' (Du Boulay, 1974: 37). In short, she says 'people did not live by money, but by land'.

Caroline Humphrey in her recent study of the Lhomi of north-east Nepal has encountered similar attitudes to money. These peoples use money infrequently, and treat it as a windfall when they acquire some (Humphrey, 1985: 67). For the most part they barter for the common products that they seek through exchange. A Lhomi counts himself rich by virtue of ownership of land, livestock, and valuables such as jewellery. Money, when it is obtained, is turned into goods which are invariably deployed in village feasts. Old Indian rupees are sown onto women's hats as indications of wealth. Silver coins until recently were melted down to make bracelets and belts. 'The expectation that in the future one will be poorer, not richer, and that other people also will be poorer, which is the Lhomi experience of the past decades, inclines people to prefer the immediacy of barter' (Humphrey, 1958: 63). In barter the money exchanged for a valuable comes to have something of the valuable about it. According to Humphrey, this is because the mentality of the barter is one of equal exchange. Moreover, in a barter economy, having money rather than goods may put someone at an advantage, and thus in an unequal position. She argues as a result that barter does not necessarily give rise to monetarization in a society such as the Lhomi, but money may be treated as goods which are bartered. As in Greece and Turkey, 20 and 30 years ago, so in north-east Nepal today, money circulates slowly, barely with the velocity described for Late Saxon England.

The circulation of coins in medieval Europe is difficult to estimate. There were undeniably many millions of pennies minted by Late Saxon kings, and many more millions were being issued by the fifteenth century (cf. Grierson, 1975). But who was using them and where? Contemporary sources leave us in no doubt that cash was used in later medieval towns. Market transactions were made using coins; services were bought using coins; waged labour gradually evolved with currency providing the key to its existence. One illustration of the important role of money is the opposition to its use. Jacques Le Goff has drawn attention to the taboo on money as its invasion of the economy grew stronger. Theologians like the twelfth-century St. Bernard of Clairvaux cursed it and aroused hostility against merchants – who were set upon as usurers (Le Goff, 1980: 60). Medieval texts are hard on champions who faced ordeals for a fee in place of the person concerned, and on prostitutes, 'an extreme case of *turpe lucrum*, ill-gotten gains' (1980: 60). Le Goff is particularly interesting on Italy's later medieval universities where academic expenses were debated as hotly as they are today, and where fees, exchange-rates and credit were matters of great concern (Le Goff, 1980: 101–06). But did the people denied history have access to money?

When one of the great sarsen stones in Avebury's prehistoric stone circle was being moved and collapsed it crushed a man with a purse full of coins. This thirteenth-century victim was probably a minor surgeon lending a hand when his fate was sealed. Coins, however, occur sparingly in all West European archaeological excavations of later medieval sites. As a rule slightly more buckles, brooches and imported honestones, for example, will be found in the average town or rural site than coins. Nevertheless, peasant houses appear to produce roughly similar numbers of coins as castles or town houses.

(Sadly, no available statistics exist as yet to confirm this assertion, though the documentary references to coinage are numerous.)

It is tempting to conclude, therefore, that money was used commonly in later medieval Europe in all spheres of society. Equally, it would be logical to conclude that it was treated as bullion in the sense that it was seldom lost, and was deployed to obtain commodities like buckles, brooches and honestones which could not be made in domestic circumstances. Nevertheless, it would be wrong to suggest that Europe as a whole uniformly accustomed itself to the use of coins. Coinage was absent from first-millennium Ireland altogether, and was then sporadically introduced to the Norse communities in the eleventh and twelfth centuries, before the Anglo-Norman invasion. After this English moneyers issued coins on behalf of the colonial power which circulated widely within the eastern, richer half of the country, but occur rarely in the West. Barter was presumably the principal mechanism of exchange outside the anglicized areas. Bartering, of course, remained an important medium of exchange in wealthier and more advanced regions of medieval Europe as well. Over 350 runic inscriptions from twelfth- and thirteenth-century Bergen show that it was of paramount importance in international business transactions. The inscriptions bear notes on the bartering of corn, winter-cod, cod-liver oil, pepper ('Thorkel the coiner sends you pepper'), salt, ale, mead, yarn ('These threads are Solveig's') and so forth. These tally-sticks, like the linear B tablets of the Minoan palaces, provide an index of the careful calculations made of resources in precapitalist societies where coinage was absent or uncommon. Even so, a strong suspicion exists that in most parts of Europe, late medieval society was conditioned to use cash in a way which those twentieth-century Polish, Turkish and Greek peasants found unacceptable. Charles the Great's early ninth-century promulgations urging the Franks to use currency, like the Late Saxon laws issued by West Saxon kings depict an understanding of coinage as a valuable agent of commerce.

The large numbers of coins associated with the first generation of England's Late Saxon competitive markets implies that silver pennies were freely circulating and were freely lost as prices fluctuated wildly with the formation of new economic conditions. Subsequent attitudes to cash in most feudal territories of Western Europe, it might be argued, were embedded in the makings of this tradition.

But was money important enough to generate class divisions in Western Europe before the end of the thirteenth century? Lester K. Little believes it was. Little (1978: 34) reminds us once more of the two sides of money: its functional portability facilitated individual mobility as well as the patronage of the Church; yet it contributed to the shift of values in the medieval world as kinship was replaced by service as the dominant relationship within society. The Church could benefit from monetization, but morality declined as wealth gradually became measured in terms of things. This step towards capitalism was not favoured by staunch churchmen. Whereas depictions of royal and imperial coins were used to decorate sacred books of the ninth and tenth centuries, some 300 years later apes defecating coins made their appearance in the margins of gothic manuscripts. Money was commonly portrayed as filthy, and associated with excrement. As Little points out, Freud directed modern attention to the same association. Attitudes to money of this kind, it seems, belong to the moment that a complex feudal society finally begins to shed the morality of a tribal age.

# 5

# Markets and their regions

Few peasants in the modern world are untouched by marketing, and by a pricing mechanism that determines the value of their products, labour, land and capital. Peasants in the past were also affected by their relations with markets. In Polanyi's opinion, once the institution of market exchange came into being it had bearing on most aspects of the lives of not only urban but also rural communities. But it is clear from a century of debate that peasants have been and are affected differently by the existence of this institution. Often peasants have suffered at the hands of the market, while for some, market integration has brought great advantages. In large measure the influence of the market is determined by the structure of the broader economy, by the variation in the type of market that engages peasants rather than the degree to which peasants engage in a market. This theme has seldom been explored in these terms. Instead, peasant marketing has been investigated from the standpoint of the individual community (the Little Tradition, as Robert Redfield described it) or conversely in overviews that necessarily depend upon those sources provided by the people who made history rather than those (in Eric Wolf's terms) without it.

It is often assumed that price-making markets have invariant properties that automatically transform traditional/under-developed economies into developed ones. Peasant economies accordingly tend to be located on a continuum of market penetration, normally at a midway point (as was noted in chapter 1). But the mechanisms of market exchange are clearly not as straightforward as they might appear. A market system involves prices and the distribution of factors of production – labour, land, capital – which are historically affected by other factors outside the economic system. To begin with it is the prices of these factors that determine the prices of the commodities exchanged in the market and not the prices of commodities which determine factor prices. With time, of course, commodity prices feed back into factor prices, but the initial fabric of trade is determined by the costs of production incurred by the parties involved. As Carol A. Smith has stated: 'The price-making market . . . is part of a sociocultural system in which factor ownership and factor scarcities determine the conditions of exchange, and these are determined by nonmarket forces' (1977: 119). The influence of the market and commodity circulation/consumption, in particular, cannot be divorced from the organization of the factor market, in other words from those who have access to the means of production. Put simply, a factor market will be competitive only if the commodity market is competitive, and vice versa. If we follow the logic of central-place theory proposed by Christaller, and advanced more recently by Smith (see chapters 1–3), the factor and commodity markets will be embodied in the regional patterning of rural marketplaces. It follows, therefore, that the influence of the market on peasant communities will be significantly different in regions where, for example, either a dendritic or a solar central-place pattern exists.

In this chapter I wish to explore this theme in three different contexts. First, the classical world offers an intriguing forum in which to examine the role of the consumer city, as Moses Finley has described it, and its influence upon its region. Most archaeologists and historians would concur with Finley's thesis that Roman towns were not primarily centres of production and distribution. Whether in Roman Italy or Roman Britain they were prominent places of administration and the implementation of imperial order. In other words they were principally solar central-places (where $k = 7$), to use the terminology employed throughout this book. By contrast, the

medieval peasant market constitutes a familiar (if controversial) expression of what George Dalton terms a traditional
market system where we can judge the influence of interlocking competitive marketplaces as opposed to the monopolistic variant typical of classical antiquity. Lastly, it is
pertinent to review briefly the influence of modern peasant
market systems in terms of their influence upon their regions.
This is the place to dwell momentarily on the influence of the
market on households, drawing a little upon the wealth of data
available from many Redfieldian studies. In this analysis,
though, it behoves us to reflect critically upon the position of
these households in a world system which has utterly different
socio-economic configurations from that of either its classical
or medieval forebears.

## Traditional systems

The role of peasant markets in the ancient and medieval
worlds has come under increasing scrutiny in recent years. In
both historical arenas there are those (in the footsteps of Marx)
who advance the view that commodity circulation was highly
restricted and those who oppose this thesis. Increasingly
this has become a subject of wider enquiry as historians and
others seek to explain the 'European Miracle' (the Industrial
Revolution/the rise of capitalism) (Jones, 1981) or, conversely,
the uniqueness of the East (Wickham, 1985). Following in
Max Weber's footsteps there has been a growing understanding
that nearly two millennia of history shaped the birth of the
industrial revolution and the capitalist tradition inherent to it.
The role of market forces in the formation of a West European
social ethos, is a signally important dimension of this history.

Historians of the ancient world are as polarized as any about
the place of the market in regional economies. Marx, as we
have noted already, believed that the town was a separate
entity in Roman society. The corollary of this is to postulate
that the countryside was populated by a slave-owning elite

who also maintained town-houses. In Marx's sketchy view, Roman society was fatally divided and herein were the seeds of its ultimate catastrophe. It is a view currently elaborated by G. de St. Croix in a grand panoramic account of the classical world (1981) and from a different and inimitable standpoint by the eminent Italian archaeologist, Andrea Carandini (1985). There is something rather operatic about these caricatures of the Roman age, and it is hardly surprising that they have been substantively challenged (Finley, 1985b). Archaeologists of Roman Britain, by contrast, have tended to over-emphasize town and country relations. In the footsteps of Adam Smith, it has been commonplace to illustrate the incidence of ranked markets within the various regions of this distant province of the Empire (cf. Hodder, 1972).

This deduction founded upon archaeological evidence may to some extent account for the late Moses Finley's lack of sympathy for history's discomforting sister discipline! Finley, as might be expected, has formulated an attractive third alternative appraisal of the classical town and its regional influence. Finley has laid claim to Weber's thesis on the ancient city as a centre of consumption rather than a place of production or exchange. He advances the argument that the Roman town was the product of an imperial system rooted in its agrarian economy. It contained administrators and an elite who owned the great ranches and estates. This type of city, as Finley defines it, was not full of merchants, marketeers, artisans and their workshop assistants. Instead it was typically a place of monumental buildings with sufficient service industries (to borrow modern terminology) to survive in a largely separated domain from its regional resource base.

Even the archaeology of towns and industrialism in a far-flung province like Roman Britain reinforces this point. Roman Cirencester, London and Winchester were very different from their medieval counterparts. Even a provincial town was dominated by its public buildings and facilities and little of its precious space was allocated to artisans. Instead craftsmen were aggregated in their own villages or unwalled towns. The potters of the New Forest and the Nene Valley or the leadworkers of the Mendips are illustrations of the separation of town, industry and the population. Crafts were primarily practised where the resources were to be found as opposed to where their products might be exchanged. To emphasize this point Finley tellingly reminds us of the differences between the ancient and medieval towns: 'it seems commonly overlooked that the excavators of Tarsus have found no Cloth Hall, that all ancient cities lacked the Guildhalls and Bourses which, next to the cathedrals, are to this day the architectural glories of the great medieval cities of Italy, France, Flanders, the Hansa towns, or England. Contrast the Athenian Agora with the Grande Place in Brussels' (Finley, 1981: 18). To reinforce this point, he observes that such was the character of the Roman city that it decayed 'so badly' as to require a second rise of towns in the Middle Ages.

These three disparate positions on the ancient town have come under scrutiny as a new source of data about the ancient world has come to light far from the ancient town itself. Modern deep-ploughing has revealed the great density of classical smallholdings dotted about the Roman Empire. Archaeologists have systematically recorded these rather ephemeral remains in virtually every province of the Empire. This field evidence brings the lot of the peasant-farmer firmly into the debate about the ancient economy, though historians have yet to assimilate fully the implications of these discoveries. Put briefly, smallholdings (the equivalent of dispersed cottages) are the most prominent settlement type in the Empire between the first and third centuries AD. In most provinces holdings of this kind are positioned at about kilometre intervals in Italy, coastal North Africa, Spain, France, much of Britain). In more marginal landscapes, for example, in the pre-Sahara of Libya or upland Britain the density is not so great and the settlements are of a more nucleated character. Who exactly occupied these prodigiously common dwellings, and what impact did solar central-places, if that is what ancient cities were, have upon their inhabitants?

Archaeology is unlikely to tell us about the institutional status of these dispersed holdings. It will not categorically indicate whether they were for example, slave-holdings or tenant farms. Peter Garnsey, however, in an essay evaluating the historical significance of these recent archaeological discoveries in Italy advances the view that these were peasants, in many cases the homes of tenants tied to great estates (1979). Garnsey also draws attention to the different regional patterning of peasant proprietors in the Italian peninsula. Historical factors played an important part in this patterning, but so too did economic factors such as the nature of the agrarian resource base. Garnsey also examines the place of the town in terms of these smallholdings. He shows how large numbers of families are recorded (and sometimes moved) in the territory of regional towns. Clearly some peasant families lived in these towns and worked smallholdings within an immediate catchment. The majority, however, were dispersed to fill up the wider expanses of the town's administrative territory. Hence, according to Garnsey, there were urban-based agricultural workers in Pompeii. Likewise Virgil's old Corycian farmed a few *iugera* under the citadel of Tarentum. Nevertheless, these were probably the exception rather than the rule. But was the norm a gentleman such as Lucius Calidius Eroticus, a resident of a rural centre in Samnium (in Central Italy) who is depicted on a funeral relief from Aesernia? Apparently he has come into town and is seen paying his bill for a bed at an inn, a flagon of wine and a girl. He is wearing a countryman's cloak and leading a mule. In Garnsey's opinion he exemplifies 'the well-attested role of the ancient city as regional market, religious and recreational centre' (1979: 18). How does archaeology support this interpretation?

Lucius Calidius Eroticus is unlikely to have inhabited one of the prodigious number of smallholdings described above. More probably he inhabited a *villa rustica* – a country house by any modern definition, and a place denoting some accumulated wealth. Less probably, he occupied a farm within the immediate environs of the town – a cottage of some kind. The vast majority of the small farms within the territories of towns like Aesernia are by medieval and modern standards strikingly impoverished in material terms. These were modestly-built structures, seemingly little more than simple prefabricated houses in modern terms, with a conspicuously limited array of ceramic tablewares, no evidence of finer articles such as glassware and few extra-regional utilitarian items such as quernstones and honestones. Personal ornaments, too, are remarkably rare. As yet, it has to be emphasized that the data relating to these places are still unsatisfactorily poor; too few classical archaeologists have appreciated the significance of these modest remains. But at face value the range and quality of articles are far fewer than those occurring on medieval sites. In this respect we can consider the theses advanced about the role of the towns as markets. The circulation of basic commodities to households of this status appears to have been highly inefficient and in marked contrast to the abundant material wealth of those large and small villas for which the world of Roman archaeology is better known. The evidence, tentative as it is, contradicts the Adam Smith thesis quite categorically. The very existence of these cottages challenges the traditional Marxist appraisal, and in broad terms these simple sites add some fresh perspective to Finley's thesis.

At present it appears that the influence of the market and its economy were to some extent limited within the classical age by the political structure of the Empire. The reasons for this are complex and beyond the realms of this book. But one corollary in some provinces was the growth of periodic markets to serve rural households. The significance of these is difficult to assess. Another corollary, as Finley indicates, is that the ancient economy and its political nuclei were vulnerable to volatile change. The collapse of the Roman Empire appears to have been far more complete, to judge from recent archaeological research, than some historians have believed. In particular, the peasantry appear to have virtually evaporated, to the consternation of archaeologists and historians alike, such was their tenuous place in society. As we shall see later in this chapter, these are conditions not altogether different from those shared by many peasantries of recent times. In short, the political status of markets, reflected in the structure of regional settlement systems, can be far-reaching.

The place of the market in medieval society has been debated along much the same lines as its role in antiquity. In this context, though, no-one questions the prominent place of markets as centres of trade and production in the Middle Ages. Indeed, as Jacques Le Goff shows, the history of the Middle Ages is to some significant degree embodied in the changing attitude of the Church to marketing and production as the feudal order was correspondingly eroded (1980: 58–70). Hence, Gilles le Muisit's *Dit des Marchands*, a fourteenth-century poem, sums up a common conviction (Le Goff, 1980: 66):

> For itself no country can provide;
> For that merchants travel far and wide;
> Their work and toil feeds the nation
> So refrain from baseless fulmination.
> Merchants cross the seas and back
> To bring each nation what it lacks
> No good merchant would reap blame
> But love, honour, and just a good name.
> They contribute to the love of nations
> Thus their wealth is cause for jubilations
> A good trader's ruin is cause for pity
> May their souls see the light of the Heavenly City.

The archaeology of the great European ports as well as inland market towns endorses the theme of this Flemish poem. The public buildings of medieval towns were far fewer than in the ancient world, and in cases like the great cathedral of Chartres or the splendid guild halls and market halls of the Flemish cities, temples dedicated to their merchants and artisans. Workshops and warehouses constituted a large part of the fabric of these towns. But to what extent did these ranked markets with their traders and craftsmen have an influence upon the rural communities within their vicinity? Here lies an opportunity to examine the impact of competitive interlocking market systems on (in the words of Rodney Hilton) one of the 'most thoroughly investigated of all peasantries in history' (Hilton, 1973: 10).

Historians are famously divided about the role of the market in this society. Recently a series of debates, promoted by the periodical *Past and Present*, has scrutinized the influence of markets and, in particular, the circulation of commodities (Hilton, 1978; Macfarlane, 1978; Aston and Philpin, 1985). Neoclassical economists, for example, have dissected the available evidence for thirteenth-century England as if they were examining the present public lending borrowing sector (cf. North & Thomas, 1973). Others have followed Marx in emphasizing the divisions within society, and its economic implications. However, although scholars are divided in their interpretations of the medieval market, none go so far as to claim that peasants practised a closed household economy. Few, moreover, would assert that English or Continental European peasants in this period were constrained by those difficult circumstances that Alexander Chayanov ascribed to post-Revolution peasants in Russia (see chapter 2). Scholars as diametrically opposed as Michael Postan (1975: 135) and Rodney Hilton (1973: 6-7) are in agreement that the medieval peasant's life was not one of pitiless drudgery. The medieval market played a prominent part in European society. In the case of thirteenth-century England manorial court rolls, for instance, point to market forces operating in patterns of intra-village debt, in the pattern of migrations to and from villages and in the different levels of rents and wages near market centres (Smith, 1979; Dyer, 1980). But the inland market towns (the intermediate markets of G. W. Skinner's typology) of late medieval England remain shrouded in sufficient mystery (in contrast to the great ports like Bristol, London, Lynn and Southampton) to sustain a considerable modern antipathy, for example, to the thesis that market forces structured the regional configurations of the age.

A stimulating new dimension to his debate has been introduced by Alan Macfarlane in his book *The Origins of English Individualism* (1978). Macfarlane focuses upon family structures and their implications for property development and social transition. He draws a distinction, rather as George Dalton has done (1972), between the classical peasantries of Asia and Eastern Europe and the West European peasantry (Macfarlane, 1978: 32–3). The constraints imposed upon classical peasantries, manifested for example in their restricted access to commodities are largely attributed to the multiple inheritance systems practised in these societies. This creates, in Macfarlane's opinion, the Redfieldian distinction between the Great Tradition (of the pan-national, general, religious, political and legal order) and the Little Tradition of the local community. In Western Europe (with certain exceptions like Ireland) the single-heir scheme of inheritance produced an altogether different social trajectory in which a significant dialectic – mediated to some extent by the marketplace – existed between the Great and Little Traditions. Macfarlane, accordingly, challenges the prevailing paradigm that late medieval England was a peasant society. He exposes the inherent weaknesses of the documentary sources and proceeds to review a range of data to illustrate the property-owning rights of many peasants as well as their access to commodities. The individualism embodied in the English family – a feature of the Industrial Revolution, and a feature in Marc Bloch's opinion of the unusual strain of English feudalism – should be traced back to the High Middle Ages. As a result Macfarlane disputes Rodney Hilton's assertion that the prominence of thirteenth-century peasant markets relates to a mere episode brought about by population pressure (Hilton, 1974: 39; Macfarlane, 1978: 194). In particular, he disputes the belief that there was in England a gradual evolution from a 'peasant' to an 'industrial' family structure. Progress as such cannot be reduced to these terms. But Macfarlane acknowledges that he cannot pinpoint the origins of these socio-economic circumstances and moreover, it could be said that the documentary sources, such as they are, can cut both ways.

To assign the origins of this social condition to thirteenth century England begs many questions (White and Vann, 1983; Smith, 1984). It necessarily concentrates attention upon the passing of the Norman and Angevin feudal order as well as the growth of the medieval world economy (cf. Schneider, 1977). This is tantamount to using Hilton's argument for the episodic short-term florescence of market towns. Macfarlane, in fact, makes no strong plea for a thirteenth-century starting-point and admits, instead, that this is merely the limit of his knowledge. It would appear that another Whig horizon has coloured his interpretation: 1066. To what extent did the Normans impose a feudal order thereby altering the shape of the Anglo-Saxon realm? J. C. Holt, analyzing the history of the elite, argues that 1066 was a threshold of change (1982). By contrast, H. R. Loyn has recently contended that the Normans made full use of the existing Anglo-Saxon political fabric, usurping in effect the reins of power (1984). It is certainly consistent with the Norman achievement in other parts of Europe (Douglas, 1970). But we should not disregard the fact that the Norman Conquest occurred as the economic structure of Europe was beginning to adapt to greater integration than it had known since the brief Carolingian episode (Hodges & Whitehouse, 1983), and in real terms since the fourth century. As Fernand Braudel has noted, it is to this age that we can attribute the roots of the modern world economy (1984). Competitive markets and the widespread use of early cash were a prominent feature of this age. On the eve and in the wake of this transition the archaeological evidence indicates that the political order of the English was becoming more stratified. Kinship was being replaced by service as an important relation within society. At the same time, as we have noted in the preceding chapters, it is archaeologically apparent that the circulation of early cash and manufactured commodities was extending far beyond market towns (Sawyer,

1965; Hodges, 1988a). Yet in this transformation of English society, the archaeology leads us to be suspicious of great changes in the peasant family structure. Moreover, through integration into the burgeoning regional economies of England, the peasantry appeared to prosper rather than suffer from the division of classes. In other words the archaeological evidence points to the broad outlines of the family structure to which Macfarlane attaches great importance being in place in England before the turn of the millennium.

In England the first regional systems of competitive, inter-locking markets accommodated traders and craftsmen. Tenth-century charters and wills as well as the laws of the age bear witness to the productive character of the towns. Public buildings were few by comparison with their Roman counter-parts. The pattern of towns and, similarly the dense pattern of urban mints in many of them, indicate the royal policy of managing urban development in Late Saxon England (Hodges, 1982). The archaeological evidence, however, points to the predominantly insular character of this market evolution, with precious little evidence for international trade before the early to mid-eleventh century. Archaeology also points to the origins of these market-places as centres of production in the pre-state emporia of the late seventh to ninth centuries (see chapter 3). The widespread distribution of manufactured commodities, therefore, appears to be a characteristic of the earliest competitive market systems, and there is no sound archaeological reason to suppose that this pattern altered over the next five centuries. Indeed, quite the reverse: recent studies of late medieval (thirteenth- to fifteenth-century) pottery production have emphasized the highly efficient marketing strategies of these low-status artisans. Potters in the Weald, in the West Midlands and in North Yorkshire, to take just three areas, manufactured and distributed a great array of wares. Excavations of deserted medieval villages, for example, have revealed that their occupants had had access to surprising amounts of utilitarian as well as prestige tablewares. Likewise higher status metal containers appear to have been widely

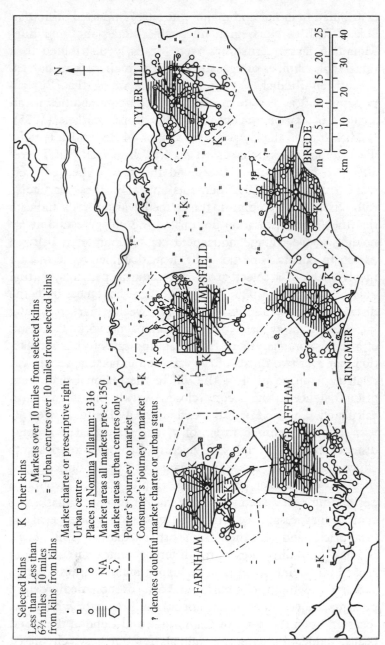

**Figure 11**  *The marketing of late medieval pottery in south-east England.  Source: Streeten 1981.*

Selected kilns    K  Other kilns

Less than    Less than    - Markets over 10 miles from selected kilns
6⅔ miles    10 miles    = Urban centres over 10 miles from selected kilns
from kilns    from kilns

·    □    Market charter or prescriptive right
○    ○    Urban centre
NA    Places in <u>Nomina Villarum</u>: 1316
‖‖‖    Market areas all markets pre-c. 1350
⬡    Market areas urban centres only
       Potter's 'journey' to market
       Consumer's 'journey' to market    = K
⌀    denotes doubtful market charter or urban status

TYLER HILL

BREDE

LIMPSFIELD

RINGMER

GRAFFHAM

FARNHAM

N

m  0    5    10    15    20    25
km  0    10    20    30    40

distributed to minor and major elite sites. Imported utilitarian objects such as Norwegian mica-schist honestones and Eifel Mountain lava quernstones were similarly distributed to a remarkable number of peasant as well as higher-status homes.

Kathleen Biddick has reinforced the thesis that English peasants had access to market-produced commodities in an analysis of thirteenth-century Bedfordshire markets (1985). Biddick studied the lay subsidy rolls for 44 Bedfordshire vills. Two to four villagers assessed the wealth in each vill. Thereafter two chief county taxers and the sheriff checked their work. In all some 1,050 peasants appear in these particular rolls. In Biddick's opinion these 'medieval tax rolls indicate that they (these peasants) dominated the village economy by holding above-average household capital and often being a patron to clients. The tax roll, then, documents the market involvement of a select group of medieval peasants, virtual kulaks' (Biddick, 1985: 826). Biddick has measured the distance of each vill to its three closest weekly markets, taking into account the available communications' network. The result of a regression analysis of these data indicates to her satisfaction that over two-thirds of the variation in taxable wealth was related to the position of the vill in the regional marketing grid. Distance to the second closest weekly market was also calculated. This revealed that each of the 44 Bedfordshire vills was situated within 6 miles of a market, with the average distance being 3.7 miles. Evidently Bedfordshire peasants enjoyed a more or less equal chance of buying or selling at their closest market. As Biddick rightly notes, 'favourable positioning near a second weekly market increased marketing choices for peasants, contributed to their knowledge about local prices, and kept their transport costs down' (1985: 827). Biddick also illustrates how different grains circulated in ranked marketing spheres. The luxury malting grains, barley and dredge (a mixture of barley and oats) of these Bedfordshire peasants, moved in an international market sector which was focussed upon the ports of Cambridge and London. Peas and beans, fodder for fattening animals for butchery, circulated in inter-regional, regional and local market sectors. Rye and oats, also used as animal fodder, circulated in regional and local markets respectively. As Biddick observes, the market geography of these different malting and fodder grains draw attention to a hierarchy of marketing choices open to the peasants. Biddick reinforces this appraisal of the market geography with telling reference to the pattern of cattle wealth, also the subject of assessment in these tax rolls.

'Market forces organized the age cohorts of the herd. Holdings in young cattle declined with distance from regional centres and from major roads. Peasants kept young stock near major towns, which required provisioning with meat. Holdings in mature working stock, representing a greater capital investment, concentrated around the inter-regional centre of Cambridge, to which capital flowed, and presumably around which peasants farmed more intensively.' (Biddick, 1985: 830).

In Biddick's opinion, such was the economic sphere inscribed by the market system upon the medieval peasantry that they buffered themselves against potential fluctuations by scattering their plots of land within the common field systems. Communal efforts to minimize risk, however, were bound to mediate against the fullest penetration of the medieval market system. Similarly bread wheats for local markets were grown as a safeguard against the vicissitudes of the international market in the lucrative malting grains.

But while this Bedfordshire evidence adds support to Macfarlane's thesis, we must nevertheless wonder whether he has overemphasized the peculiar English characteristics to the detriment of his West European peasant model. The archaeology of Western Europe between AD 1000–1500 largely serves to endorse the model already glimpsed in England. Towns clearly evolved as centres of production and distribution - in striking contrast, as Finley observed, to their ancient forebears. Moreover, commodities circulated widely and in great numbers to the villages within their localities in quantities that often (as in southern French and Italian villages) put the English evidence into a shadow. The material wealth of the late medieval peasantry from Denmark to Italy is beyond doubt, and in the latter case makes a striking contrast with the lot of the Roman peasantry.

It would be a grave mistake, however, to assert that market development occurred uniformly in concert with the evolution of the medieval world economy. The pattern, in fact, was determined by history and by political as well as geographical factors. Hence, for example, Anders Andrén in his analysis of the 'urban scene' in Denmark asserts that the town was the product of several discontinuous processes (1985). In the main he believes the first towns were royal fiscs (in the period 1000–1200) which were gradually opened up to a feudal elite (cf. chapter 3); thereafter, between 1200–1350 towns obtained some internal independence and their regional influence on society took a new direction. But, in Andrén's opinion, the medieval town only gained an identity of its own in the great age of the Hanseatic League when these places were liberated from feudal fiscal deliminations and influenced by the passage of pan-European socio-economic events. Andrén's overview takes little account of the production and distribution of commodities. Instead, he focuses upon church building as an index of development. His measure is to some extent confirmed by the late development of low-grade industries like pottery-production – an industry that evolved slowly in comparison to the circumstances in England. This urban scene, however, must be attributed to Denmark's position and, in particular, to the late formation of the state. Almost until AD 1000 it was prehistoric in many of its characteristics (Randsborg, 1980), and its transformation owed much to West European 'core' influence.

In Italy at about AD 1000, with few exceptions, urbanism and the articulation of the rural resource base were remarkably less developed than in England. But the impact of the Mediterranean economy swiftly altered this condition. Historians have documented the growth of regions like Tuscany, showing the deep-rooted beginnings of the Renaissance. Their conclusions are endorsed by recent archaeological research. The peasant dwellings of the period of *incastellamento* (the tenth-eleventh centuries) appear to have been little different from the Roman peasant cottages described earlier in this chapter. Likewise the first church in the coastal village of Scarlino was a rudimentary affair (Francovich, 1988). But the second phase of these villages imitate the changes occurring in towns like Pisa during the eleventh century. The finely-built tower houses and romanesque churches became models for the villages in their territories by AD 1200. The tablewares of the merchants and artisans had been adopted by peasant families in houses nestling below feudal towers. By the thirteenth century the volume of moveable goods manufactured in regional and sub-regional markets had attained a peak which was sustained for several generations before declining in the post-medieval age. A peasant's household in central Tuscany could be mistaken for a lord's manor in the Midlands of England.

On the western rim of a world economy in which Tuscany was at the centre was Greenland. Writing in the thirteenth century, one author ascribed the colonization of this perilous country to 'a desire for gain; for men seek wealth wherever they have heard that gain is to be gotten, though on the other hand there may be great dangers too. But in Greenland . . . whatever comes from other lands is high in price, for the land is so distant from other lands that men seldom visit it. And everything that is needed to improve the land must be purchased abroad, both iron and all the timber' (*King's Mirror*, c. 1217-60, cited by McGovern, 1985: 275). Thomas McGovern has charted a fascinating relationship between this peripheral territory and the European core. The Greenlandic settlement was a risky gamble made by a collection of smallholders. McGovern, however, demonstrates from many lines of evidence (faunal species ratios, location, cattle-byre and storage shed sizes, imported artefacts and written sources) that the Norse society became increasingly hierarchical. The erosion of independence is traced to those who commanded the most productive patches of pastures. Gradually Greenlandic trade became a royal monopoly with the bishops acting as royal agents. McGovern argues (1985: 310) that the church farm of Herjolfsnes 0111 in the extreme south-west acted as a dendritic central-place, while the episcopal manor at Gardar 047 was the colony's solar central-place. This primacy, according to McGovern, can be demonstrated by the disproportionately large and numerous buildings for storage. The elite, in other words, rigorously exercised control over the flow of goods from the distant European core.

Excavations and written sources, however, show that the Greenlandic peasants failed to challenge this autonomy by allying themselves with the native Thule Inuit. The Church discouraged the use of Inuit hunting techniques and technology, consigning the Norse to a desperately maladaptive strategy with the onset of the Little Ice Age. Here, on the edge of the world the descendents of the Vinland adventure encapsulated those rigorous feudal notions challenged in the provinces of Western Europe. Regulated by a European administrative authority, espousing European church designs and even dress styles, these colonists faced extinction as the cost of trading with them became too great. Greenland is almost the exception: a medieval region where the fate of the peasantry grew harsher as the influence of the market increased. But undeniably the Greenlanders constitute a strange medieval episode, prefiguring those Third World communities manipulated by the growth of the modern world system.

*The Little Tradition*

The influence of the market in the modern world system concerned Marx and has continued to disturb anthropologists and historians. The historiography of this phenomenon has taken a western historical stance, allowing little for the diverse social and economic conditions prevailing outside this orbit. Anthropological accounts of the impact of the market on modern peasantries puts western attitudes to markets in perspective. If they call into question our values they will force us to do greater justice to the past as well as the present. It seems pertinent to explore this theme in two post-classical/ post-medieval communities – in Turkey and Greece – where market development has only just begun to alter the little tradition.

Paul Stirling's detailed account of a Turkish village in 1949–50 conjures up images that are steadily becoming as remote as any medieval ones. The great socio-economic changes of the post-war world have abraded the communal isolation he describes. His account, nevertheless, is typical of those studies of what Redfield described as the Little Tradition.

Stirling studied the villages of Elbasi and Sakaltutan in central Anatolia. These were comparatively remote communities, only recently joined to the nearest provincial town by a rough road. Sakaltutan was of medium size – about 100 households and just over 600 people. Elbasi was unusually large with over 200 households and about 1,200 people. Both villages practised extensive cultivation of cereals, mainly rye and wheat.

Stirling believes that before about 1925 little was sold or bought for cash by any but the most prosperous and powerful villagers in Elbasi and Sakaltutan.

With more land per household, supplies per head of staple grains and milk and meat products must normally have formed a larger part of a less varied diet. More clothes were produced in rural areas. Bride price was paid in gold and silver currency, and wealth was stored in gold coins worn as ornaments by the women. On the whole, most villagers marketed little direct, and most of what they did market was bartered with visiting traders for various necessities; or sold to the tax collectors; or to village leaders who could organize expeditions large enough to be safe (Stirling, 1965: 73).

For considerable periods, according to Stirling, these two villages survived without towns. What the householders could not produce they went without. When Stirling was doing his fieldwork matters had altered, largely due to the advent of motorized transport. Nevertheless, the householders still produced the greater part of what they needed.

All cereals, milk products, meat and eggs, and some at least of the fruit and vegetables consumed are produced in the village. The villages also supply their own fuel from straw, dung and scrub, build their own houses with local stone . . . breed most of their own draught animals, and satisfy their own needs for *kilims*, bags and sacks. Some of these needs are met by a small amount of trade between villages, but in most of these items each village, and to some extent each household is self-sufficient. The villagers exaggerated this self-sufficiency, and liked to emphasise their independence; in their still traditional view of the world, the land gave an assurance of survival which such unreliable sources of income as a government salary did not (p. 79).

Village craftsmen met many communal needs, though some required imported raw materials for making their tools and utensils. These craftsmen were supplemented by visiting craftsmen and by journeymen who brought ready-made goods direct from urban shops. By 1950 village imports had become considerable. Fruit, vegetables (especially cabbage and beet, which were stored and eaten during the winter) tea, coffee, *helva*, sweets, ready-made clothes, shoes, bedding, paraffin for lighting and luxury commodities like torches, bicycles, radios, watches etc. Above all lorries, flour mill machinery, fuel and spare parts had become major items for certain households.

In 1950 three or four lorries passed through Sakaltutan every day heading for the market town at Kayseri 14 miles away. (The road was constructed in the 1940's.) Kayseri then had a population of 65,000 and was linked by rail and road to Ankara and Istanbul. This connection evidently transformed village life. Traditional water-powered mills had been used to process the cereals which formed the staple of the village economy. But in the wake of the road came diesel-powered flour mills. A diesel-powered mill was set up in a nearby village in the late forties; another was purchased by the men of Suleymanli, a neighbouring village in 1950; Sakaltutan gained one in 1951 and in 1952 a migrant, returned from Argentina, built another between Sakaltutan and Elbasi. Most of these lorries and mills were afforded by favourable loans from banks. Stirling's conclusion of these investments are particularly interesting:

It is often said . . . that, like other so-called under-developed low income countries, Turkey lacks capital. Yet the rate of economic development in these villages was restricted far more by inexperience and technical ignorance than by shortage of capital, and also perhaps by fear of regulation and bureaucratic interference. If there had been clear opportunities for profit, in enterprises in which villagers felt they had the necessary experience, then a much higher rate of investment would have been forthcoming. On the other hand their expectations of profit are high (p. 72).

The impact of the wider market meant that money was a regular part of life in the village, and in 1950 every household had urgent cash needs. Almost everyone, accordingly, had a powerful stake in the grain export. Thus, each year as the harvesting ended, the lorries ran flat-out journeys to the government's grain agency. 'At the depot, officials examine each sack for quality and dampness, and eternal wrangles go on over the grading, which determines the price. In spite of these disputes, and although the grading appears to depend on the officials' personal judgement, I never heard of any villagers complaining of corruption' (p. 73).

In addition, some peasants intermittently sold potatoes, onions and ground peas in the market at Kayseri. Some also made carpets, rugs and bags for retail shops in Kayseri. One man told Stirling that years before he had taken cattle by train to Istanbul. But an incident like this as well as the return of men who had emigrated to find work were exceptions. For the most part the village was tied by its staples rather than these other products destined for the market. It was tied too by government agencies, by the advent of schooling and by a host of other social reforms that linked the hitherto divorced town and country. Stirling, like many anthropologists encountering change in hitherto isolated communities, offers an almost elegiac assessment of the increasing impact of the world and market economy upon these communities.

'By greatly increasing the range of social relations even the poorer villagers have with people outside the village it has decreased the solidarity of the village, weakening the strength of the social controls on which village conservatism is founded. The villagers are no longer necessarily dependent on their leaders . . . This process so far is no more than begun, but it has already brought the village into the nation in a much more definite and inescapable way. Even if he pays his taxes without argument and keeps out of the way when involved in violence, the villager can no longer hope to ignore the authorities. He is constantly, through the radio, reminded that he and his village are a part of a much larger social unit, the nation . . . Once the village was a social foothill to the distant urban peaks, proud in its semi-autonomy and more or less able to ignore them by looking the other way. Its social world was centred on itself. Now it is acutely aware that it is only the peripheral lower slopes, uncomfortably forced to face or evade the constant stream of interference and scorn which pours down from the urban peaks of national power.

The old attitudes are not gone. The village is still proud . . . and at times writes town society off as corrupt and decadent. But contradictions are a normal part of any society, and the opposite is heard even more often – that the village is backward, uncouth, poor, dirty and violent. Such contradictions can, of course, live more or less permanently in a society. But though I have no empirical first-hand evidence of the village attitudes two generations ago, I am confident that its pride and independent spirit are declining and its diffidence and sense of inferiority increasing (Stirling, 1965: 292-3).

Stirling's images, especially when encountered in the field, leave one pondering the dilemma imposed by the market. The cocooned solidarity of village life appears immeasurably more attractive than the unattainable affluence (as Sahlins describes it) on offer in the supermarket. Juliet Du Boulay confronted the same dilemma in the village of Ambeli – a dying village community, as she calls it – in Euboea, Greece. Here, insulated from the fast-developing world of the sixties, the remaining villagers lamented the migration of younger folk to the towns or to other countries, yet maintained an attitude to the influence of those towns which is common to most traditional modern peasantries.

Du Boulay describes it as follows:

For the villager the spending of money to buy commodities to bring into the house is not thought of in at all the same way as is the direct storing of the house with its farm produce. The villager is used to his labour resulting in two different types of acquisition - cash or kind - and he looks on work as something which should bring one or other *into the house*. If, however, the cash that is earned by the family labour is immediately expended, even though the result of that expenditure is to stock the house with something vital, a different process has taken place - one that is less satisfactory to traditional village thinking and which could almost be described as dissipation rather than conservation. The difference therefore to the villager between bringing in his foodstuffs straight from the fields to the house, and spending money to buy those foodstuffs, may be summarized as in the first instance vital commodities being brought into the house, and, in the second, a vital commodity leaving it.

The difference is not a rational one, but rational argument of a kind which deals only with material experience is a way of thought which is not used by the traditional villager to order all his actions, but only some of them, and many of his actions depend also on the way in which he perceives his relation to the natural and spiritual world which are so vital a part of his cosmology (Du Boulay, 1974: 36).

The paradox, as Du Boulay points out, is that the villagers of Ambeli, like those studied by Stirling in Anatolia, on the one hand distrust the hurly-burly of towns, while on the other sensing that urban values are necessary for a decent life (1974: 46-7). These were the last generation of Ambeli to have a way of life which was automatically in tune with the natural rhythms of the physical world and its recurrent cycle of birth, fruition, death and re-birth. Merchants' time, a feature of the inexorable development of the medieval world (Le Goff, 1980), has imposed its indelible rhythm even in this remote mountain corner . . .

# 6

# The peasant market and its extinction

Many of the distinctive features of our civilisation were formed during the 5,000 years of agrarian states. Far from being the enlightened offspring of industrialism that we fondly imagine ourselves to be, we are rather the confused by-product of social and technical processes whose implications are masked by the persistence of preindustrial cultural assumptions and institutions. There can be little doubt that the legacy of agrarian society is unravelling before our eyes; but we need the benefit of long-run, wide-angle vision - of an anthropological vision - if we are to have much chance of sorting out the elements of the era our generations are setting in train.

K. Hart, *Heads or tails? Two sides of the coin.*

Medieval markets, of course, are extinct. But their siblings, those primitive and peasant markets in the Third World that in many cases have become indices of poverty, live on. To the tourist these places are superficially exciting and colourful, as Sidney Mintz illustrates in the quotation at the beginning of this book. But in reality while medieval markets figured prominently in the transition to capitalism, these Third World variants are anachronisms.

The markets of the Third World remind one to some extent of the Greenlanders in Renaissance times - marginal actors on the rim of the great wheel of modern capitalism. But unlike the Norse in Greenland these actors constitute a majority in global demographic terms of those engaged in market exchange. Put in these terms one may readily concur with the findings of the Brandt commission on International Development when it asserts that the 'world community faces much greater dangers than at any time since the Second World War' (Brandt, 1980: 267).

The debates about terminology and approaches to economic anthropology have masked the power of the data assembled since Malinowski's time. Formalists, substantivists and Neo-Marxist French structuralists have more in common than they often choose to indicate. Like historians, they have a place in the future of the globe. The global revolution in progress needs its scientists every bit as much as England did in the eighteenth century. In economic affairs, it is simply not sufficient to concentrate our energies upon the future of capitalism - an issue that galvanizes the First World. The future of the globe depends upon appreciating axioms as simple as those outlined by John H. Dowling (see chapter 1). The need to meet 'infinite wants', to satisfy social strategies as well as regional peculiarities require resource planning on the scale envisaged by Willy Brandt and his colleagues. This utopia, as in medieval times, depends upon direction. Like many historical geographers, I assert that these political conditions are manifested in the material expressions of their economic relations: in the form of their market systems. The use of space as a resource provides images of the past which should inform us on the direction of our destiny.

This is particularly clear, for example, when we examine the fate of the Roman Empire. Rostovtzeff asked of it: 'Why was the victorious advance of capitalism stopped? Why was machinery not invented? Why were the business systems not perfected? Why were the primal forces of primitive economy not overcome?' (1957: 538). The answers, of course, will not be provided by the ruins of Roman consumer cities (as Finley called them) or by the prolific numbers of impoverished farmsteads dotted throughout the imperial provinces. These are images of how it was. But the images reveal an economic inefficiency, and in particular a malaise in the classical production-distribution systems. The images are measures of a social order ill-prepared to administer a community as grand as this was.

A markedly different image underpins the West in medieval times. As we have seen in the foregoing chapters, Europe experienced a primeval period after the demise of the Roman Empire before its market institutions were aroused once again. The combination of a prehistoric social order and classical science was certainly important in the rebirth of towns. The sequence of pre-market institutions, in fact, paved the way to the emergence of competitive markets in the tenth and eleventh centuries. The sequence appears to rest upon the evolution of stratified social systems. Nation-states, in other words, needed a high energy infrastructure to maintain the political machinery. Yet the apparent paradox is that the divisions which galvanized Marx's attention are barely comparable to those which sealed the fate of classical antiquity. On the contrary, the history of the Middle Ages in one respect is a history of increasing access to the market-place, and the expanding influence of regional exchange.

Was the peasant market the prime mover behind the European Miracle? Or are its configurations expressions of deeper rooted relations? Writing of these circumstances in England, Richard Smith comments: 'In reality, because of the integration of its institutions, English rural society was neither in a state of Hobbesian "warre" nor a geographical scattering of small, introspective corporate republics waiting to be integrated into a larger body politic by the outward-orientated "middling sorts" . . . (Instead, there was a) long-term dialectic of economic individualism and political and philosophical collectivism that exists as a recurring theme. . . .' (Smith, 1984: 178-9). The transition from feudalism to capitalism was complex and must be viewed in systemic rather than monocausal terms. In the debate amongst Marxist historians on this matter some looked to the role of traders and the explicit growth of the market, others looked to the aspirations of landed lords and others attempted to analyze the part played by the peasantry. Paul Sweezy, for example, identified Mediterranean merchant capital as the agent of change in later medieval England (and Europe). In his opinion, the mechanisms of change did not exist within the feudal mode which he regarded as static and self-perpetuating (1976). The archaeological evidence to some extent confirms the thread of his argument: merchant capital was being accumulated in thirteenth-century North Sea ports, and was altering the pattern of urban production and distribution as well as inducing changes in rural attitudes to production and distribution (cf. Davey & Hodges, 1983). But was it a prime mover?

Rodney Hilton argued that the necessary if fluctuating pressure by the ruling class for the transfer to itself of peasant surpluses was the essential cause of the technical progress and improved feudal organization which made for the enlargement of the available surplus. In Hilton's opinion this was the basis for the growth of simple commodity production, seigneurial incomes in cash, international luxury trade and urbanization. In these circumstances Hilton pays special attention to the efforts of the peasants to retain for themselves as much as possible of the surplus (Hilton, 1976). Hilton's view, as we saw in chapter 5, is to some extent borne out by the evidence Biddick presents in the case of Bedfordshire peasants. But archaeology illustrates that commodity circulation did not just begin as feudalism waned and capitalism took shape. The roots of commodity circulation lie in the formation of the European markets. Also the roots of the social relations, to which Richard Smith refers, lie in these times. The growth of the European economy and the evolution of its society went hand in hand. When we examine the archaeology of the transition to capitalism it is the integrated, systemic character of later medieval Europe that distinguishes it from the Roman Empire. In short, Smith's, Sweezy's and Hilton's theses are dimensions of a many-faceted whole. England and Europe forged their own social character from the crucible of classical collapse. They also forged a new world-economy which brought a new rhythm to the pattern of socio-economic development. But that rhythm had limited impact upon the southern and eastern shores of the Mediterranean, whereas its reception in North-west Europe formed part of a more complex social patterning.

This point is summed up within the Italian peninsula where the two patterns met. The wealth of the Tuscan peasantry, described in the foregoing chapter, contrasts markedly with the abject poverty of the later medieval peasantry in the Kingdom of Naples. Their resource base was similar; if anything the classical and early medieval history of the latter was richer, but the roots of what Carlo Levi described as the 'Other Italy' came about as the medieval world-economy took shape with Tuscany forming part of its heartland, while in the Kingdom of Naples resources were concentrated rather than circulated. In short, attitudes to marketing offer a measure of the transition to modernity. The growth of industrial towns is obviously a direct reflection of this European transition. But in many ways a more telling manifestation of the beginnings of capitalism is to be found in the fields of England and other European countries. As the new towns needed increased rural output, it became necessary to reorganize agrarian production. New fields, hedges, walls and millions of miles of field drains are one manifestation of this transition. Equally, and more pertinent, the ubiquitous sherds of mass-produced drinking pots and pitchers belonging to this age reflect not only the growth of mass-production but the circulation of such commodities to all corners of these nations. Hence, alongside the newly-built drystone walls of eighteenth-century Derbyshire, farmhands dropped mugs and cheap porcelein plates. Such was the momentum of this industry that the same objects accompanied George Washington's men as they pushed through the woodlands to found forts in their confrontation with the French on the Ohio river.

The condition of the Third World lies in its history – in its different trajectory to that ascribed to the English, for example, by Richard Smith – and in the huge momentum of the modern world system as the globe has shrunk in size and as the appetite for resources for the First World has generated quixotic expansion in the Third World. On the one hand

**Figure 12**   *A scene in the weekly (Sunday) market at Sousse, Tunisia.*
*Source: author.*

peasants like those in Anatolia and Eubeoa, described in chapter 5, have to come to terms with the market. On the other hand, the Brandt commission estimates that 800 million people inhabit regions in which inefficient market systems strive to mediate with the world economy. The tiny primate centres of Greenland have become sprawling monopolistic solar central-places and dendritic central-places connected by jet-age bankers to the first world. The confusion, as Carol A. Smith has described in the case of Guatemala, is dismaying.

It is not appropriate to tell these people to assimilate western history – to change. Malinowski was among the first anthropologists to appreciate this point. Anthropology was often funded in the thirties and forties to document colonial peoples so that they might be roped within the economic system of the western world. Development economists in many cases have advanced their work at the behest of international and national interests. But as Polly Hill shows the statistics do no justice to the circumstances; the people without history, in effect, are the subject of arbitration without representation (1986). Hill argues that gross misconceptions abound on the economics of country-people, on their household units, on their inheritance, on the role of women, on rural stratification and on demography. She traces some of these misconceptions to what she terms the vain search for universal generalizations: historicist fallacies. 'Economists' . . . dread of incomprehensible marshes of empirical detail is doubtless one of the main reasons why so many of them still cling to an historicist approach, though it is fairly commonly believed that there is simply no alternative' (1986: 51). For example, she asserts that many development economists, schooled in western historical economics, imply that capitalism is apt to creep into the countryside from the cities almost as a kind of virus. 'This is a belief which takes no account of the fact that in many tropical regions, *until quite recently*, the countryside was the matrix within which most economic enterprise flourished, most traders having been countrymen, and large cities having been rare and anomalous places; and it altogether underestimates the capacity of rural communities to innovate, both organizationally and technically, on their own initiative' (1986: 51–2). Historical fallacies, she asserts, abound and can be traced – as they can in our own history – to the straight-jacket of nineteenth-century historicist theory.

Hill rightly argues that as the art critic seldom gives practical advice to artists, so anthropologists should be wary of making practical suggestions to economists. Yet she is spurred on by 'the old-fashioned, stereotyped Western-biased, over-generalized crudity and conceptual falsity of so many conventional economic premises, as well as economists' complacent attitude to bad official statistics' (Hill, 1986: xi). Hill is putting her finger upon a malaise that still afflicts western history. Too little attention has been paid to the people who are without history; they have been slotted into a category that as much as anything is derived from Marx's restricted perspective of world history. Multi-disciplinary sources and armies of scholars afford us advantages unavailable a century ago, yet we seem chained to expedient observations of the past which take no account of our resources as historians of human behaviour. To understand the formation and mechanisms governing peasant markets seems to be of fundamental importance to the present. It tells us much about ourselves and the conditions of our world. Such history is out of fashion; some historians, according to John Hall, even consider it to be dangerous (Hall, 1985: 4). The link between applied history (if we could so term it, rather than philosophical history) and the modern world conjures up in many minds the totalitarian strategies enacted in the thirties. Yet as Polly Hill informs us, other strategies exist – indeed the Brandt commission formulated a great many. It is surely the time for those who have studied past processes in terms other than those in which western history is summed up as a moral success story with the virtuous winning out over the bad guys (to paraphrase Eric Wolf), to take a fuller part in our future.

Our future options depend upon the lucid debate of our interdisciplinary data about the past. We must convey to politicians the point that like medieval markets, those in the Third World are not 'congealed in aspic' forever. We need the benefit of long-run, wide-angle vision – of an anthropological vision – to avert catastrophes of our own making. As markets govern our lives in more ways than ever it is time to draw together the numerous threads of historical, archaeological, anthropological and sociological research to prepare a new perspective of history. In this book I hope that I have rehearsed some of the arguments for this case; but clearly it is little more than a beginning.

# Bibliography

Adams, R. McC. (1981): *Heartland of Cities: Surveys of Ancient Settlement and Land Use on the central floodplain of the Euphrates.* Chicago.

Andrén, A. (1985): *Den urbana scenen. Städer och samhälle i det medeltida Danmark.* Lund.

Aston, T. S. and Philpin, C. H. E. (1985) (eds): *The Brenner debate: agrarian class structure and economic development in pre-industrial Europe.* Cambridge.

Barker, G. (1978): Economic models for the Manekweni zimbabwe, Mozambique. *Azania,* 13, 71–100.

Bender, B. (1978): Gatherer-hunter to farmer: a social perspective. *World Archaeology,* 10, 204–22.

Biddick, K. (1985): Medieval English peasants and market involvement. *Journal of Economic History,* XLV, 823–31.

Blanton, R. (1976): Anthropological studies of cities, *Annual Review of Anthropology,* 5, 249–64.

Bloch, M. (1983): *Marxism and Anthropology.* Oxford.

Blomstrom, M. and Hettne, B. (1985): *Development Theory in Transition.* London.

Bohannan, P. and Dalton, G. (1961) (eds): *Markets in Africa.* Evanston.

Borger, H. (1985): Die Erben Roms? Die Anfange der mittelalterlichen Stadt Koln in archaologischen Sicht. *Archaologie in Deutschland,* 4, 24–7.

Bradley, R. (1984): *The Social Foundations of Prehistoric Britain.* London.

Brandt, W. (1980): *North-South: a programme for survival.* London.

Braudel, F. (1980): *On History.* London.

—— (1984): *The perspective of the world: civilisation and capitalism, 15th.-18th. century, vol. III.* London.

Brown, P. (1974): *Mohammed and Charlemagne* by Henri Pirenne. *Daedalus*, 103, 25-33.

Brughardt, A. F. (1971): A hypothesis about gateway communities. *Annals of the Association of American Geographers*, 61, 269-85.

Carandini, A. (1985): *Settefinestre. Una Villa schiavistica nell'Etruria Romana.* Modena.

Chaudhuri, K. N. (1985): *Trade and Civilization in the Indian Ocean.* Cambridge.

Chayanov, A. (1966): *The Theory of Peasant Economy.* Homewood, Illinois.

Cherry, J. F. (1978): Generalization and the archaeology of the state. In D. Green, C. Hazelgrove and M. Spriggs (eds), *Social Organization and Settlement*, Oxford, 411-37.

Chisholm, M. (1968): *Rural settlement and Land Use.* London.

Christaller, W. (1966): *Central Places in Southern Germany.* New Jersey.

Clarke, D. L. (1977): Introduction, in D. L. Clarke (ed). *Spatial Archaeology.* London, 1-32.

Collis, J. R. (1971): Functional and theoretical interpretations of British coinage. *World Archaeology* 3, 71-84.

Cowgill, G. (1975): On causes and consequences of Ancient and Modern population changes. *American Anthropologist*, 77, 505-25.

Dalton G. (1961): Economic theory and primitive society. *American Anthropologist*, 63, 1-25.

—— (1965): Primitive money. *American Anthropologist*, 67, 44-65.

—— (1972): Peasantries in Anthropology and History. *Current Anthropology*, 13, 385-416.

—— (1973): Peasant Markets. *Journal of Peasant Studies*, 1, 240-3.

—— (1975): Karl Polanyi's analysis of long-distance trade and his wider paradigm. In J. Sabloff and C. C. Lamberg-Karlovsky (eds), *Ancient Civilisation and Trade*, Albuquerque, 63-132.

—— (1977): Aboriginal economies in stateless societies. In T. K. Earle and J. Ericson (eds), *Exchange systems in prehistory*, London, 191-212.

—— (1978): Comments. In R. Hodges Ports of Trade in Early Medieval Europe, *Norwegian Archaeological Review*, 11, 97-111.

Davey, P. J. and Hodges, R. (1983): Ceramics and trade: a critique of the evidence. In P. J. Davey and R. Hodges (eds), *Ceramics and Trade*, Sheffield, 1-15.

Doran, J. (1979): Fitting models and studying process: some comments on the role of computer simulation in archaeology. *Bulletin of the Institute of Archaeology*, University of London, 16, 81-94.

Douglas, D. (1970): *The Norman Achievement*. London.

Douglas, M. (1967): Primitive rationing: a study in controlled exchange. In R. Firth (ed), *Themes in Economic Anthropology*, London, 119-47.

Dowling, J. H. (1980): The Goodfellows *vs*. The Dalton Gang: the assumptions of economic anthropology. *Journal of Anthropological Research*, 35, 292-308.

De St. Croix, G. E. M. (1981): *The Class Struggle in the Ancient Greek World*. London.

Du Boulay, J. (1974): *Portrait of a Greek mountain village*. Oxford.

Dyer, C. C. (1980): *Lords and peasants in a changing society*. Cambridge.

Earle, T. (1977): A reappraisal of redistribution: complex Hawaiian chiefdoms. In T. K. Earle and J. Ericson (eds), *Exchange Systems in Prehistory*, London, 213-29.

Eggers, H. J. (1952): *Der romische Import im freien Germanien*. Hamburg.

Finley, M. I. (1981): The Ancient City. In M. I. Finley, *Economy and Society in Ancient Greece*, London, 3-21.

Finley, M. I. (1985a): *The Ancient Economy* (second edition). London.

Finley, M. I. (1985b): *Ancient History. Evidence and Models*. London.

Firth, R. (1939): *Primitive Polynesian Economy*. London.

Firth, R. (1946): *Malay Fishermen: their peasant economy*. London.

Firth, R. (1964): Capital, saving and credit in peasant societies. In R. Firth and B. S. Yamey (eds), *Capital, Saving and Credit in Peasant societies*, London, 15-34.

Francovich, R. (1988): *Scarlino II. Scavi 1978-82*. Florence.

Flannery, K. (1972): The cultural evolution of civilisations. *Annual Review of Ecology and Systematics*, 3, 399-426.

Frank, A. G. (1966): The development of underdevelopment. *Monthly Review*, 18, 17-31.

Frankenstein, S. and Rowlands, M. J. (1978): The internal structure and regional context of early iron age society in south-western Germany. *Bulletin of the Institute of Archaeology*, University of London, 15, 73-115.

Freidel, D. A. and Sabloff, J. A. (1984): *Cozumel: Late Maya Settlement Patterns*. Orlando.

Friedman, J. and Rowlands, M. J. (1978): Notes towards an epigenetic model of the evolution of civilisation. In J. Friedman and M. J. Rowlands (eds), *The Evolution of Social Systems*, London, 201-76.

Galinie, H. (1988): Reflections on early Medieval Towns. In B. Hobley and R. Hodges (eds), *The Rise of the Town in the West, AD 700-1000*, London, forthcoming.

Garnsey, P. (1979): Where did Italian peasants live? *Proceedings of the Cambridge Philological Society*, 29, 1-25.

Giddens, A. (1981): *A contemporary critique of historical materialism*. London.

Godelier, M. (1977): *Perspectives in Marxist Anthropology*. Cambridge.

Gregory, C. A. (1980): Gifts to men and gifts to god: gift exchange and capital accumulation in contemporary Papua. *Man*, 15, 626-52.

Gregory, C. A. (1982): *Gifts and Commodities*. London.

Grierson, P. (1959): Commerce in the Dark Ages: a critique of the evidence. *Transactions of the Royal Historical Society*, 9, 123-40.

Grierson, P. (1965): Money and coinage under Charlemagne. In F. Braunfels (ed), *Karl der Grosse I*.

Grierson, P. (1975): *Numismatics*, Cambridge.

Grierson, P. and Blackburn, M. (1986): *Medieval European Coinage, volume 1; The Early Middle Ages (5th-10th centuries)*. Cambridge.

Haggett, P. (1965): *Locational Analysis in Human Geography*. London.

Hall, J. A. (1985): *Powers and Liberties*. Oxford.

Hardh, B. (1977-78): Trade and money in Scandinavia in the Viking Age. *Papers of the Lund Institute*, 2, 223-50.

Harding, T. G. (1967): *Voyagers of the Vitiaz Strait*. Seattle.

Harris, M. (1980): *Culture, People, Nature*, third edition. New York.

Hart, K. (1986): Heads or tails? Two sides of the coin. *Man*, 21, 637-56.

Harvey, P. D. A. (1985): Mapping the Village: the historical evidence. In D. Hooke (ed), *Medieval Villages*, Oxford, 33-46.

Hazelgrove, C. (1982): Wealth, prestige and power: the dynamics of late iron age political centralisation in south-east England. In C. Renfrew and S. Shennan (eds), *Ranking, Resource and Exchange*. Cambridge, 79-88.

Hedeager, L. (1979): A quantitative analysis of Roman imports in Europe north of the Limes (0-400 AD), and the question of

Romano-Germanic exchange. *New Directions in Scandinavian Archaeology*, 1, 191-216.

Heidinga, A. (1984): *Der Veluwe in de Vroege Middeleeuwen. Aspecten van de nederzettingsarcheologie van Kottwijk en zijn buren.* Amsterdam.

Herodotus (1971): *The Histories* (trans. by A. de Selincourt). Harmondsworth.

Hill, P. (1986): *Development Economics on Trial.* Cambridge.

Hilton, R. (1973): The Manor. *Journal of Peasant Studies*, 1, 107-09.

Hilton, R. (1974): *Bond Men Made Free*, London.

—— (1976) (ed) *The Transition from Feudalism to Capitalism.* London.

—— (1978): Reasons for inequality among medieval peasants. *Journal of Peasant Studies*, 5, 271-84.

Hirth, K. G. (1978): Inter-regional trade and the formation of pre-historic gateway communities. *American Antiquity*, 43, 25-45.

Hodder, I. (1972): Locational models and the study of Romano-British settlement. In D. L. Clarke (ed), *Models in Archaeology*, London, 887-909.

Hodges, R. (1978): Ports of trade in early medieval Europe. *Norwegian Archaeological Review*, 11, 97-111.

—— (1982): *Dark Age Economics.* London.

—— (1988a): *The Anglo-Saxon Achievement.* London.

—— (1988a): *A Dark Age Pompeii: San Vincenzo al Volturno.* London.

—— and Cherry, J. F. (1983): Cost-control and coinage: an archaeological approach to economic change in Anglo-Saxon England. *Research in Economic Anthropology*, 5, 131-84.

—— and Whitehouse, D. (1983): *Mohammed, Charlemagne & the Origins of Europe.* London.

Hogbin, I. (1964): *A Guadacanal Society. The Kaoka Speakers*, New York.

Holt, J. C. (1982): Feudal society and the family in early medieval England. *Transactions of the Royal Historical Society*, 32, 193-212.

Humphrey, C. (1985): Barter and economic disintegration. *Man*, 20, 48-72.

Irwin, G. (1978): Pots and entrepôts: a study of settlement, trade and the development of economic specialization in Papuan prehistory. *World Archaeology*, 9, 299-319.

Johnson, G. (1975): Locational analysis and the investigation of Urak local exchange systems. In J. A. Sabloff and C. C. Lamberg-Karlovsk (eds), *Ancient Civilisation and Trade*. Albuquerque, 285-339.

—— (1977): Aspects of regional analysis in archaeology. *Annual Review of Anthropology*, 6, 479-508.

Jones, E. L. (1981): *The European Miracle*. Cambridge.

Kraay, C. (1964): Hoards, small change and the origin of coinage. *Journal of Hellenic Studies*, 84, 76-91.

Leach, J. W. (1983): Introduction. In J. W. Leach and E. Leach (eds) *The Kula, new Perspectives on Massim Exchange*. Cambridge, 1-26.

Le Goff, J. (1980): *Time, Work, and Culture in the Middle Ages*. Chicago.

Little, L. K. (1978): *Religious poverty and the profit economy in medieval Europe*. London.

Loyn, H. R. (1984): *The Governance of Anglo-Saxon England 500-1087*. London.

Malinowski, B. (1922): *Argonauts of the Western Pacific*. London.

Marx, K. (1976): *Das Kapital*. London.

Mauss, M. (1925): *Essai sur le don*. Paris.

Macfarlane, A. (1978): *The Origins of English Individualism*. Oxford.

McGovern, T. H. (1985): The Arctic Frontier of Norse Greenland. In S. Green and S. Perlman (eds), *The Archaeology of Frontiers and Boundaries*, New York, 275-323.

Mintz, S. W. (1962): Peasant markets. *Scientific American*, 203, 112-22.

Montanari, M. (1979): *L'aliminentazione contadina nell'alto Medioevo*. Naples.

North, D. C. and Thomas, R. P. (1973): *The Rise of the Western World: A New Economic History*. New York.

Paynter, R. (1982): *Models of Spatial Inequality: Settlement Patterns in Historical Archaeology*. London.

Pirenne, H. (1925): *Medieval Cities*. Princeton.

Polanyi, K. (1957): The economy as Instituted Process. In K. Polanyi, C. Arensberg and H. Pearson (eds), *Trade and Markets in Archaic Societies*, Glencoe, 243-69.

—— (1963): Ports of trade in early societies. *Journal of Economic History*, 23, 30-45.

Postan, M. M. (1975): *The medieval economy and society*. Harmondsworth.

Porlaksson, H. Comments on Ports of Trade in Early Medieval

Europe. (1978): in Hodges, R. (1978): Ports of Trade in Early Medieval Europe, *Norwegian Archaeological Review*, 11, 112-114.

Randsborg, K. (1980): *The Viking Age in Denmark*. London.

— (1982): Ranks, rights and resources: an archaeological perspective from Denmark. In C. Renfrew and S. Shennan (eds), *Ranking, Resource and Exchange*, Cambridge, 132-9.

— (1985): Subsistence and settlement in Northern Temperate Europe in the First Millennium A.D. In G. Barker and C. Gamble (eds), *Beyond Domestication in Prehistoric Europe*, London, 233-65.

Randsborg, K. forthcoming: *From Roman Empire to Medieval Society*.

Rathje, W. L. (1975): The last tango in Mayapan; a tentative trajectory of production-distribution systems. In J. Sabloff and C. C. Lamberg-Karlovsky (eds), *Ancient Civilisation and Trade*, Albuquerque, 409-48.

— (1978) Melanesian and Australian exchange systems: a view from Mesoamerica. *Mankind*, 11, 165-74.

— and Sabloff, J. (1973): Ancient Maya commercial systems: a research design for the Island of Cozumel, Mexico. *World Archaeology*, 5, 221-31.

Renfrew, C. (1972): *The Emergence of Civilisation: the Cyclades and the Aegean in the Third Millennium B.C.* London.

— (1975): Trade as action at distance: questions of integration and communication. In J. Sabloff and C. C. Lamberg-Karlovsky (eds), *Ancient Civilisation and Trade*, Albuquerque, 3-59.

— and Cherry, J. F. (1986): (eds), *Peer-polity interaction and sociopolitical change*. Cambridge.

Rostovtzeff, M. I. (1957): *The Social and economic history of the Roman Empire*, second edition. Oxford.

Russell, J. C. (1972): *Medieval Regions and Their Cities*. Bloomington.

Sahlins, M. (1960): Political power and the economy in primitive society. In G. E. Dole and R. L. Carneiro (eds), *Essays in the Science of Culture in Honor of Leslie White*, New York, 390-415.

— (1974): *Stone Age Economics*. London.

— (1985): *Islands of History*. Chicago.

Sawyer, P. (1965): The wealth of England in the eleventh century. *Transactions of the Royal Historical Society*, 15, 145-64.

Schumpeter, J. (1954): *A history of economic analysis*. London.

Schneider, J. (1977): Was there a pre-capitalist world system? *Journal of Peasant Studies*, 6, 20-9.

Shanin, T. (1971): Peasantry as a political factor. In T. Shanin (ed), *Peasants and Peasant Societies*, Harmondsworth, 238-63.

Silverman, S. (1979): The peasant concept in anthropology. *Journal of Peasant Studies*, 6, 49-69.

Skinner, G. W. (1964-65): Marketing and social structure in rural China. *Journal of Asian Studies*, 24, 3-43; 195-228; 363-99.

—— (1976): Mobility strategies in Late Imperial China: a regional systems analysis. In C. A. Smith (ed), *Regional Analysis*, vol. i, London, 327-64.

Slofstra, J. *et al* (1982): *Het Kempenprojekt. Een regionaal-archeologisch onderzoeksprogramma*. Amsterdam.

Smith, C. A. (1976a): Exchange systems and the spatial distribution of elites: the organisation of stratification in agrarian societies. In C. A. Smith (ed), *Regional Analysis*, vol. ii, London, 309-74.

—— (1976b): Regional economic systems: linking geographical models and socioeconomic problems. In C. A. Smith (ed), *Regional Analysis*, vol. i, London, 3-63.

—— (1977): How marketing systems affect economic opportunity in agrarian societies. In R. Halperin and J. Dow (eds), *Peasant Livelihood. Studies in Economic Anthropology and Cultural Ecology*, New York, 117-46.

—— (1984): Local History in Global context: social and economic transitions in western Guatamala. *Comparative Studies in Society and History*, 26, 193-228.

Smith, R. (1979): Kin and neighbours in a thirteenth-century Suffolk community. *Journal of Family History*, 4, 285-312.

Smith, R. M. (1984): Modernisation and the corporate medieval village community in England. In A. H. Baker and D. Gregory (eds), *Explorations in Historical Geography*, Cambridge, 140-80.

Steponaitis, V. (1978): Location a theory and complex chiefdoms: a Mississippian example. In B. D. Smith (ed), *Mississippian Patterns*, London, 417-54.

Stirling, P. (1965): *A Turkish Village*. London.

Streeten, A. D. F. (1981): Craft and industry: medieval and later potters in south-east England. For H. Howard and E. Morris (eds), *Production and Distribution: a ceramic viewpoint*, Oxford, 323-46.

Sweezy, P. (1976): A critique. In R. Hilton (ed), *The Transition from Feudalism to Capitalism*, London, 33-56.

Thomas, W. I. and Znaniecki, F. (1958): *The Polish peasant in Europe and America*. New York.

Thorner, D. (1971): Peasant economy as a category in economic history. In T. Shannin (ed), *Peasants and Peasant Societies*, Harmondsworth, 202-18.

Wacher, J. (1974): *The Towns of Roman Britain*. London.

Wallerstein, I. (1974): *The Modern World System*. London.

Werner, J. (1961): Fernhandel und Naturalwirtschaft im ostlichen Merowingerreich nach archaeologischen und numismatischen Zeugnissen. *Bericht der Romisch-Germanisch Kommission*, 42, 307-46.

Wheatley, P. (1975): Satyanrta in Suvarnadvipa: from reciprocity to redistribution in ancient southeast Asia. In J. Sabloff and C. C. Lamberg-Karlovsky (eds), *Ancient Civilisation and Trade*, Albuquerque, 227-84.

Wheeler, R. E. M. (1954): *Rome beyond the Imperial Frontiers*, London.

White, S. D. and Vann, R. T. (1983): The invention of English individualism: Alan Macfarlane and the modernization of pre-modern England. *Social History*, 8, 345-63.

Wickham, C. (1985): The uniqueness of the East. *Journal of Peasant Studies*, 12, 166-96.

Winklemann, W. (1954): Eine westfälische Siedlung des 8 Jahrhunderts bei Warendorf, Kr. Warendorf. *Germania*, 32, 189-213.

Wolf, E. R. (1955): Types of Latin American peasantry. *American Anthropologist*, 57, 452-71.

—— (1966): *Peasants*. New Jersey.

—— (1972): Comments. In G. Dalton (ed), Peasantries in Anthropology and History. *Current Anthropology*, 13, 385-416.

—— (1982): *Europe and the People without History*. Berkeley.

Wright, H. T. (1983): Trade and politics in the western Indian Ocean, unpublished lecture given at SUNY-Binghamton, New York, 21/10/83.

—— and Johnson, G. (1975): Population, exchange and early state formation in southwestern Iran. *American Anthropologist*, 77, 267-89.

# Index